Arnaud's

RESTAURANT
COOKBOOK

Arnaud's
RESTAURANT
COOKBOOK

Kit Wohl

Foreword by Linda Ellerbee

PELICAN PUBLISHING COMPANY

GRETNA 2005

ISBN 9781589803091

Historical photographs courtesy of Arnaud's Restaurant Archives
and The Historic New Orleans Collection

Edited by Brigit Binns
Jacket photograph by David G. Spielman
Jacket and book design by Jedd Haas

Printed in Singapore
Published by Pelican Publishing Company, Inc.
1000 Burmaster Street, Gretna, Louisiana 70053

In honor of great ladies, our mothers:

Ellen Casbarian, Eleanor Mundt, Helen Maxey More, Mildred Wohl,

with all our love and gratitude.

Table of Contents

Introduction

Special Occasions and Spectacular Meals 28

Celebration on the Half Shell 52

Hors d'Oeuvres, Canapes and Appetizers 62

Soups and Salads 76

Brunch 92

Seafood 106

Meat and Poultry 130

The Casual Side of Creole Cooking 152

Toast the Cocktail 166

Sweet Conclusions 178

The Basics - Sauces, Stocks & Seasonings 200

Index 221

Foreword

When I come to New Orleans I check into my hotel and then go to Arnaud's. If I'm thinking straight, I go to Arnaud's before I check into the hotel and the maître d' hides my bags behind the front desk.

I go because Arnaud's celebrates the classics. Which is why it is one.

My first meal at Arnaud's was during the Louisiana World's Fair in 1984. Lunch was several dozen raw oysters followed by Shrimp Arnaud followed by Crabmeat Imperial—jumbo lumps of it and no filler. Honest food carefully prepared and elegantly presented. I sighed over my Café Brulôt. I was a fan.

Some of the Creole dishes on Arnaud's menu have been there for 85 years. According to proprietor Archie Casbarian, there never was a good reason to remove them. There are new things now too, but change is slow to come at Arnaud's. For which we may all be grateful.

What the Casbarian family has done is taken a grand old lady and returned to her all her joie de vivre. Certainly they gave her a face lift—perhaps more than a polite nip and tuck—but they have preserved what makes Arnaud's a New Orleans institution.

Few restaurants survive the first year. Even fewer make it to the five-year mark. When a restaurant celebrates 85 and is still going strong, there's something right going on. One right thing is that Arnaud's has always been a family affair. Still is. Jane and Archie Casbarian have owned it for the last 25 years. Not surprisingly, a new generation of them is now involved.

I visit Arnaud's as often as I can and have been lucky enough to become friends with Jane and Archie. There are no better reasons to come to New Orleans. Good friends. Good food.

Linda Ellerbee

Introduction

Arnaud's lasting success can be attributed in part to the consistency of its owners. It has known only two families since its establishment in 1918, from the colorful founder "Count" Arnaud Cazenave, to his equally flamboyant daughter Germaine Cazenave Wells, who followed him as proprietor, to her heir apparent, Archie A. Casbarian.

During the mid-1800s, restaurants in New Orleans graduated from cafés serving rough workingmen to establishments more suitable for ladies and gentlemen. In 1918, a colorful French wine salesman named Arnaud Cazenave opened the grand restaurant that still bears his name and is one of the few originals that survive to this day.

The choice of Archie Casbarian as Arnaud's next proprietor was as peculiar as it was propitious.

He had the same initials as the departing proprietor's father. Both men enjoyed good cigars, bespoke clothing, fine wines and especially the telling of an amusing story. Both were born overseas, and spoke French fluently. The two men were even the same height. In fact, Germaine was superstitious and thought that Casbarian looked a lot like her father.

Casbarian, with a European culinary education finished by Cornell University and refined in some of America's most spectacular hotels, brought a classical background and attitude. Jane, his wife, is a native Orleanian, and has the kind of palate that only a local could develop from years of dining in Creole restaurants and on the finest home cooking. Their combined talents revived Arnaud's from the brink of extinction.

The Casbarians were committed to the idea that the new Arnaud's should look like the old Arnaud's and not a brand-new restaurant.

The original chandeliers, iron columns and cypress paneling were restored. The old ceiling fans also stayed. The wall of opaque, pebbled glass windows overlooking Bienville Street was replaced by sparkling beveled glass. During the renovation a small section of the original tin ceiling was found, and replicated to cover the entire main dining room. Silver, glassware and china patterns selected were, by coincidence, similar to those originally chosen by the Count back in 1918.

Finally, after an initial $2.5 million investment and the blood, sweat and tears of an army of workers, the renovated main dining room and kitchen were ready.

Arnaud's renaissance was finally underway.

Twenty five years later, the next generation is already a major part of the restaurant. Brother and sister Archie, Jr. and Katy grew up at Arnaud's and held tricycle races through the main dining room.

Archie, Jr. joined the family business following his graduation from the University of Pennsylvania and has worked both in the back and front of the house.

After three years in New York City at the Waldorf-Astoria Hotel as well in the kitchen of restaurateur and chef Daniel Boulud, Katy returned home to join her family at Arnaud's. She graduated from Cornell School of Hospitality and Hotel Management, her father's alma mater.

Family celebrates opening night at Arnaud's:(left to right) Ellen Casbarian, matriarch of the Casbarian clan; Archie and Jane Casbarian, proprietors; Dr. Leslie and Eleanor Mundt, Jane's parents; and Peter Casbarian, Archie's brother. Not pictured: Peter's wife, Karen; the third Casbarian son, John, and his wife, Natalye Appel; and patriarch Ohan Casbarian.

Real Creole

Casbarian insists that, while new dishes are essential to the restaurant's growth, they must fit in with the Creole cuisine for which Arnaud's is celebrated.

Creole is the ethnic food of New Orleans, and it dominates the local culinary scene the way French food does in France or Italian food does in Italy. Creole is to the city as Cajun is to the bayou countryside.

It grew from a grafting, two centuries ago, of French dishes onto African cooking practices, with Spanish, Italian, German and American influences. The oldest and best-developed of American regional cooking, Creole is unique.

Creole food is always full-flavored, with generous components of butter, pepper, salt and herbs. The combination of onions, bell peppers and celery, cooked in a Roux of oil and flour, is the starting point for a tremendous number of Creole dishes, although Creole tastes can also emerge when none of these ingredients are present. The one essential is flavor, and plenty of it. It is a misconception that Creole food is peppery hot. Certainly it can be spicy, but in the well seasoned sense, as the result of a careful blend of herbs and spices.

A spicy bite should be relieved by something mild on the palate, Casbarian believes, each in harmony with the wine, then savory against sweet. One course should follow another in a balancing act of contrast, taste and texture.

Traditions

A restaurant as venerable as Arnaud's has quirky ways of doing things. Casbarian, a traditionalist, holds dear the small rituals and courtesies that distinguish his establishment. Consider the cap bread: it is a twisted and knobby chunk of fresh French bread, baked daily, only for Arnaud's. Each table is presented with a loaf, warm and crisp, gift-wrapped in a white linen napkin. Guests are encouraged to litter the tablecloth with crumbs. Breaking bread together is a tradition and making crumbs is part of it. These breadcrumbs require Arnaud's waiters to carry a peculiar little tool called a crumber. The crumber is used to tidy the table throughout the meal by scraping the crumbs into a small pile and then ceremoniously whisking them away.

The Count

Count Arnaud, as he came to be called, began with a small restaurant and bar, now the old Absinthe House at Bourbon and Bienville; it stands catty-corner from Arnaud's. Because of the restaurant's success, his establishment quickly outgrew the original premises and in 1920 was moved across the street to a larger building, a former warehouse refitted as a restaurant, in the center of Bienville Street.

The restaurant's popularity grew from the Count's personality and beliefs. He believed that the pleasures of the table were as worthy as anything else one chose to pursue in life. For him, a simple, less-than-festive meal was a shamefully wasted opportunity for making life better. This concept played well to celebration-minded Orleanians, who instantly took Count Arnaud to their hearts.

He always printed his philosophy of dining on Arnaud's menus.

"When choosing a New Orleans Restaurant—a dinner chosen according to one's needs, tastes and moods, well prepared and well served, is a joy to all senses and an impelling incentive to sound sleep, good health and long life. Therefore, at least once a day, preferably in the cool and quiet of the evening, one should throw all care to the winds, relax completely and dine leisurely and well. Au revoir, mes amis! Je vais vivre at diner en sage."   Arnaud Cazenave (1876-1948)

Another of the Count's observations:

"New Orleans, justly termed the "Paris of America," has also the distinction of being the Second Port in the New World; but we may add safely and without boasting that it stands second to none in the variety and excellence of its food."

Generations of guests have made Arnaud's an important part of their family histories. It is considered the place to bring a child for his or her first grown-up meal in public. Romantics all, the staff love engagements, rehearsal dinners and wedding parties. Birthdays, anniversaries and other major family events are an occasion for joy all around.

Throughout the restaurant there are oddities that have not changed since they were instituted. The old brass coat hooks are still useful for hanging coats, canes and shopping bags.

Carafes at each table are a salute to the days when water was not so readily available, much less labeled by brand and sold in fancy bottles.

The Count (left) entertains Bob Hope, two unidentified friends and New York City Mayor Fiorello La Guardia (far right) following an interview on WWL radio during a visit to New Orleans. WWL is still on the air.

This menu, dating from the early 1930s, contains many dishes that are still available at Arnaud's such as Shrimp Arnaud, Trout Meunière, Chicken Clemenceau, Bonne Femme and Rochambeau, Oysters Rockefeller, Brochette and Suzette, Seafood Courtbouillon, Eggs Benedict, Brabant Potatoes and Baked Alaska. Shrimp Arnaud was the first item on that menu. It is still first on the menu.

The menus created by the Count were vast and varied. One listed nine oyster appetizers, 51 seafood entrees and 40 vegetables (among them potatoes prepared 16 ways). This extravagant list wasn't just for show; every dish was available. These menus defined French-Creole cuisine for decades. He used his menus to communicate attitudes and observations about the world of fine dining.

In the 1930s and '40s, Arnaud's was the undisputed leader of New Orleans restaurants. It was the venue for any occasion that demanded celebration and the prime rendezvous for Canal Street businessmen; over Arnaud's special lunches, their regular tables were lively with conversation and commerce.

Dinner at the legendary restaurant was *de rigueur* for everyone who was anyone. Arnaud's has enjoyed more than its share of celebrity fans over the decades; in the era of the Count and Germaine, the dining rooms were graced by Loretta Young, Tom Mix, a very young Bob Hope, Arthur Godfrey, Errol Flynn and many others.

THE COUNT'S MENU COMMENTARY

IMPORTANT! TO OUR GUESTS

"We mean no offense…but in these strange, disturbing days of ultra money consciousness, we feel that the following hint of caution is not extremely out of place:

"We serve special lunches and dinners daily at popular prices. These are what we call the bargains of the restaurant industry… but remember that when you order a la carte you pay for each article separately excepting bread and butter.

"It requires a great deal of extra help in the kitchen and an extensive stock of goods on hand to do justice to this sort of service. We have reduced many articles as much as possible. Nevertheless, to avoid painful surprises, look over the menu prices carefully before ordering. The waiter or headwaiter will help you as far as portions are concerned."

Carte Du Jour

Relishes

mps Arnaud	.40	Crab Meat Canapé	.50
hovy Canapé	.40	Crab Meat Canapé with Anchovies	.60
de á l'Imperiale	.50	Caviar Canapé	.70
quettes, Lucille	.60	Avocado, Alicia	.75
ry Stuffed with Roquefort	.50	Avocado Cocktail	.25
Pasto (per tin)	.50	Canapé de Foie Gras	.50
ines, Imported (per tin)	.50	Canapé Savarin	.60
fed Crab, Ravigote (Cold)	.50	Olives, Green or Ripe	.25
ato Juice	.20	Stuffed Olives	.25
ur d'Artichaut, Princesse Louise	.50	Tomato a l'Imperiale	.50

Oysters

ters, ½ Shell	(½ doz.) .30	Oysters, Rockefeller	(½ doz.)	.50
Fried or broiled	" .30	Suzette	"	.50
Coquille	" .50	Whitney	"	.50
Brochette	" .50	Poulette	"	.50

Shell Fish

e Shrimps, Plain	.40	Crab Meat, Cocktail	.30
Cocktail	.30	Coquille	.50
Fried, Tartar Sauce	.50	Gratin	.60
Créole and Rice	.50	St. Pierre	.60
Poulette	.75	Newburg	.75
Newburg	.75	Soft Shell Crabs, Fried or Broiled	
er Shrimps, Plain	.50	Busters, Fried or Broiled	
Cocktail	.40	Meuniere	
fed Crab	.40	Armandine	
a la Diable	.50	Crayfish	

Potages

p du Jour	.15	Turtle Soup	.25
ter Soup (½ Doz.)	.30	Créole Gumbo	.30
on Soup, Gratin	.30	Cream of Tomatoes	.25
on Soup, Gratin with Egg	.40	Cream of Asparagus	.30
somme, Hot or Frappé	.20	Crayfish Bisque (Evelyn)	.30

Fish

derloin Trout, Broiled or Fried,		Pompano, Broiled	.80
Tartar Sauce	.40	Meuniere	.85
Meuniere	.50	Papillote	1.00
Meuniere Armandine	.65	Pontchartrain	
Marguery	.75	Sheepshead, Broiled	.50
Gratin	.90	Hollandaise	.85
White Wine Sauce	.90	Red Snapper Steak, Broiled	.50
Coquille	.40	Courtbouillon	.70
ssed Cold Fish, Ravigote	.35	Bouillabaisse	1.00
nish Mackerel	.50		

Eggs

n and Eggs	.40	Eggs, St. Denis	.60
on and Eggs	.40	Benedict	.60
s, Fried, Boiled or Shirred	.30	Marie	.60
Black Butter	.40	A la Normande	.60
Poached	.40	A la Turque	.60
Purgatoire	.50	A la Florentine	.60
Scrambled with Brains	.50	A la Portugaise	.50

Omelettes

elette, Oyster	.50	Omelette, Bonne Femme	.50
Spanish	.50	Cheese	.40
Purgatoire	.60	Sweetbreads	.50
Fine Herbes	.35	Peas and Mushrooms	.50

Steaks

oin Steak	1.00	Tenderloin Steak,	1.25
Bordelaise Créole	1.20	Bordelaise	1.40
Marchand de Vin	1.25	Marchand de Vin	1.50
Mushrooms	1.30	Mushrooms	1.50
Fresh Mushrooms	1.40	Fresh Mushrooms	1.65
Bearnaise	1.40	Bearnaise	1.65
Stanley	1.40	Périgueux	1.65
Anchovy Butter	1.25	Anchovy Butter	1.50
Cepes Bordelaise	1.60	Cepes Bordelaise	1.85
Financiere	1.40	Filet Mignon Vera Nell	1.25
ute Steak, Brabant Potatoes	.85	Steak, Tartare	.75
nburger Steak, Brabant Potatoes	.75	Tamerlane	1.00

Double Steak—Double Price

Chops

nb Chops (2)	.90	Veal Chop, Fried or Broiled (1)	.40
With Peas	1.10	Meuniere	.50
With Peas, Francaise	1.20	Mushrooms	.65
Mushrooms	1.15	Fresh Mushrooms	.80
Fresh Mushrooms	1.30	Peas	.60
Papillote	1.25	Peas, Francaise	.70
Milanaise	1.30	Holstein	.65
glish Mutton Chops, Cumberland	1.25	Vienna Schnitzel	.60

Potatoes

French Fried	.15	Soufflée	.40
Brabant	.15	Gratin	.30
Julienne	.15	Hash Brown	.15
Sauté	.15	O'Brien	.25
Lyonnaise	.20	German Fried	.15
Cottage Fried	.20	Saratoga	.20

Fowl

Spring		Spring	
Chicken, Fried or Broiled	.80	Chicken, Bonne Femme	1.00
Meuniere	.90	Spaghetti Italienne	1.15
Bordelaise	.90	Milanaise	1.35
Creole and Rice	1.10	Maison d'Or	1.40
Mushrooms	1.15	Marchand de Vin	1.00
Fresh Mushrooms	1.20	Chicken a la King	.90
Currie Indienne	1.10	Rochambeau	.90
Cepes Bordelaise	1.40	en Coquille	.75
en Papillote	1.25	Roast Turkey, Cranberry Sauce	.75
Clemenceau	1.40	Stuffed Wings, Beatrice	.60

Plats Divers

Ham or Bacon	.40	Chicken Liver. Sauté	.60
Ham, Parisienne	.50	Brochette	.70
Champagne Sauce	.60	Italienne	.75
Kidney, Broiled	.40	Cocotte	.80
Bacon	.50	Mushrooms	.80
with Mushrooms	.60	Sweetbreads, Broiled or Sauté	.50
A la Diable	.50	Saute with Mushrooms	.65
Calf Liver, Broiled	.40	Irma	.75
Bacon	.60	Cepes Bordelaise	.75
With Onions	.60	Fresh Mushrooms on Toast	.50
Meuniere	.60	Waldorf	.75
Bordelaise	.60	Calf's Brains, Beune Noir	.50
Sphaghetti Italienne	.40	Ravigote (Cold)	.60
Meat Balls (2)	.60	Breaded, Tomato Sauce	.60
Milanaise	.50	Boiled Beef and Vegetable	.50
Meat Balls	.70	Scotch Woodcock	.50
Welsh Rarebit	.50		

Vegetables

Asparagus	.50	Tomatoes, Fried, Boiled or Stewed	.30
Cream Sauce	.60	Artichokes	.30
Hollandaise	.70	Hollandaise	.50
Asparagus Tips	.35	Carrots a la Vichy	.35
Hollandaise	.50	Brocolis and Butter	.40
Cauliflower	.50	Hollandaise	.60
Gratin	.65	French Peas	.20
Hollandaise	.70	Francaise	.30
Brussels Sprouts	.40	String Beans	.25
Hollandaise	.60	Butter Beans	.25
Fried Onions	.30	Spinach	.25
Egg Plants, Boiled or Fried	.30	Flageolets	.30

Cheese

Roquefort and Jelly	.35	Camembert and Jelly	.35
New York Cream and Jelly	.30	Domestic Cheese and Jelly	.20
		Cheese a la Waldorf	.45

Entremets

Ice Cream	.15	Banana Flambies	.60
Coupe Germaine	.40	Crepe Suzette	.75
Pudding, Cream Sauce	.15	Jelly Omelette	.40
Lost Bread	.40	Fig Omelette	.50
French Pan Cakes (2)	.35	Fritters	.40
Jelly	.40	Fruit Omelet	.50
Baked Alaska	.75	Coffe or Tea	.10
Supreme	.90	With Cream	.15
Omelette Soufflée (for 2)	1.25	Chocolate or Cocoa	.15
Supreme	1.50	Dry Toast	.10
50c Extra for Each Added Person		Buttered Toast	.15

Salads

Hearts of Lettuce	.20	Faucon Salad	.35
Tomatoes	.20	Waldorf Salad	.50
Mixed Salad	.30	Fruit Salad	.40
Potato Salad	.15	Grape Fruit Salad	.25
Beet Salad	.20	Vegetable Salad	.40
Celery Salad	.20	Cauliflower Salad	.40
Alligator Pear ½	.30	Shrimp Salad	.40
Salad	.20	Crab Meat Salad	.40
Roquefort Dressing, Extra	.25	Chicken Salad	.50
Russian Dressing, with Caviar, Extra	.50	Manuel Salad (for 2)	.80

The space grew as adjacent buildings were incorporated into the restaurant. The Count added different kinds of dining rooms throughout the complex, ranging in size from the grand second-floor ballroom with its wall-to-wall dance floor to small, elegant chambers more suited for quiet assignations.

The 1920 Room (right) was so named to mark Arnaud's move to its present location and has long been a favorite for intimate dinner parties of 2 to 12 guests.

A call button was used to summon a waiter. Guests took full advantage of the serpentine network of passageways as a means of maintaining absolute discretion. The call buttons are still in working order.

Executive chef Tommy DiGiovanni, (left) a native Orleanian, has spent most of his life in a kitchen and his creations represent the epitome of classic Creole, French and Italian cooking.

Madame Pierre was Arnaud's first chef in 1918. She was proficient in both French and Spanish cookery.

After leaving Arnaud's to gain more experience, chef Tommy returned a few years later and was greeted with a crisp new white coat. A banner stretched across the kitchen was emblazoned "Welcome Home, Tommy."

Casbarian redesigned the enormous, superbly equipped kitchen. Sous chef José Manguia keeps the cooking line moving and inspects dishes prior to their presentation at table.

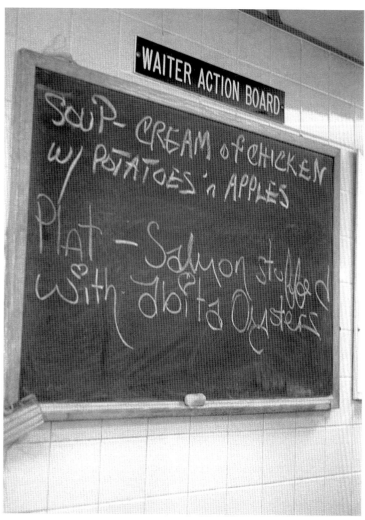

Communication is simple.

Just before showtime: a peaceful interlude for setting tables and preparing for the next meal service.

Crystal must be polished, napkins folded, silverware inspected, fresh flowers placed on each table and votive candles lighted in welcome.

Staff meals give everyone a chance to visit before the first guests arrive. The cook assigned to prepare them is careful not to incur the wrath of hungry co-workers, who are quick to point out any shortcomings in the meal.

Casbarian nurtures talent and Arnaud's staff alumni are excellent examples of such a success-based philosophy. As the result of Arnaud's rigorous training, discipline and encouragement, hostesses, waiters, cooks and other employees have gone on to complete college and graduate degrees, become president of companies, open their own restaurants and much more.

Special Occasions and Spectacular Meals

Just about the time the renovation of Arnaud's main dining room and kitchen was coming to a close, internationally noted connoisseur and wine collector Lloyd Flatt decided a magnum of 1929 Chateau d'Yquem, a dessert wine, should be consumed. Flatt was eager to taste a bottle of one of the rarest wines in the world. And Casbarian was anxious to put his new staff to work.

The two connoisseurs decided that Flatt would bring the wine, Casbarian was to provide the food and service. Casbarian, challenged to create a grand meal to accompany a great wine, began planning backwards. Usually served with dessert, Chateau d'Yquem is France's first and only great growth Sauternes that is classified as Premiere Grand Cru.

"Chateau d'Yquem ages superbly," noted Flatt as he began the ceremony of decanting the rare bottle. "It can always be drunk when young, however, and at the age of three already possesses the extravagance of perfection that begins even as the grapes are hand picked and individually snipped from the cluster."

Decanting a great wine is a delicate proposition which requires a steady hand and a keen eye. Improperly handled, sediment collected at the bottom of the bottle over the years can be disturbed, contaminating the wine, which is suspended above the dregs.

The menu, served in high style and accompanied by some of the world's finest wines, was an Arnaud's classic and the first meal served by the restaurant under Casbarian's hand.

Menu

Saturday, February 3, 1979

Mr. and Mrs. Archie A. Casbarian   Mr. and Mrs. Lloyd Flatt

Mr. and Mrs. William J. Wohl

Joseph Drouhin 1976 Meursault   Shrimp Arnaud

1971 Corton bottled by Bouchard Pere & Fils, Hospices de Beaune
Filet Charlemond

Joseph Drouhin 1976 Meursault   Pompano en Croûte

1929 Chateau d'Yquem   Crème Brûlée

A STANZA FROM THE POEM INSCRIBED IN THE CELLARS OF CHATEAU D'YQUEM

"ITS WINE IS THE HEART OF MY SENSES"

"ONLY THE GODS, OUR LADIES AND WE MAY DRINK IT;

THE GODS STANDING UP, THE LADIES SITTING DOWN,

AND WE ON OUR KNEES."

Flatt provided the theme for an off-the-corridor ramshackle linen pantry turned tiny dining room, by supplying a Methuselah of 1796 Napoleon brandy (which equals six bottles or eight liters) and other spectacularly impressive bottles to line the walls.

When he changed residences in the 1990s, Flatt moved his cellar away from New Orleans and the room was redecorated. Jane Casbarian commissioned New Orleans' artist George Dureau to create a painting of Bacchus—the Greek God of Wine— specifically for the space. Seating only eight guests, the room is in popular demand as a private, yet open room for people watching.

Filet Charlemond

In order to present the beef at its tender juicy best, cook the filets at the last possible moment. Because Charlemond Sauce is so rich and flavorful, you may want to simply sear the filets to the preferred temperature without seasoning.

6 slices beef filet, about 5 ounces each, cut 1-1/2 to 2 inches thick, patted dry with
    paper towels
Kosher or sea salt and freshly ground black pepper (optional)
1/4 to 1/3 cup clarified butter (see page 206)
Charlemond Sauce (recipe at right), hot, for serving

Preheat the oven to its lowest setting and place a serving platter and six dinner plates inside to warm.

Place a large skillet over medium-high heat and add the clarified butter. When it is very hot, add filets to the pan, as many as 3 if they are to be cooked to the same degree. Sear quickly on both sides, about 2 minutes per side for medium rare, 2-1/2 minutes per side for medium (longer cooking is not recommended.) Transfer to the platter in the warm oven. Add butter to the pan if needed and cook the remaining filets in the same way.

To serve: Make a pool of Charlemond Sauce on each plate and position a filet in the center.

Charlemond Sauce

YIELD: ABOUT 1-1/2 CUPS

1 tablespoon unsalted butter
1 small shallot, very finely chopped
3 green onions, white and light green parts only, finely chopped
1/4 pound sliced white mushrooms
1 Bouquet Garni (see page 217)
1 small clove garlic, very finely chopped
1/2 cup dry white wine
Blond Roux made with 2 tablespoons butter and 2 tablespoons flour (see page 216)
Kosher or sea salt and white pepper, preferably freshly ground
1 cup heavy cream
1/2 teaspoon granulated chicken bouillon (optional)

Place a large saucepan over medium heat and add the butter. When the foam begins to subside, add the shallot and green onions and cook, stirring occasionally, until softened and translucent, 5 to 6 minutes. Add the mushrooms and cook for 3 minutes more, until tender.

Add the bouquet garni, garlic and white wine and bring to a simmer. Cook until the wine has reduced by about half and the mixture is slightly juicy. Strain the liquid into a clean saucepan and set aside, reserving the shallot-mushroom mixture in the strainer separately. Discard the bouquet garni.

In a small pan, make the Roux as directed on page 216. Cook until thick, but not at all brown.

Add the cream and the chicken bouillon, if using, to the reduced wine, then use a whisk to blend in the Roux until smooth. Season with a pinch each of salt and pepper. Bring to a boil over medium heat and cook, stirring occasionally, until thickened. Return the mushrooms and onions to the sauce, taste for seasoning and adjust as necessary. Lower heat to very low and simmer the sauce partially covered for 4 to 5 minutes, to marry the flavors.

Pompano en Croûte

Pompano en Croûte is topped with scallop mousse then encased in a delicate puff pastry shaped like a miniature, perfectly browned fish, complete with fins and scales. It was Casbarian's first entry on the new menu.

Pompano is a truly magnificent local fin fish that is pulled from our own Gulf waters. The light white meat is slightly oily, which keeps it wonderfully moist and tender in grilled, sautéed and baked dishes. It quickly become one of the most popular dishes.

1-1/2 pounds medium scallops, very cold
1 small carrot, finely chopped
2 stalks celery, finely chopped
1 shallot, finely chopped
2 tablespoon heavy cream
3 large eggs, lightly beaten
1 teaspoon Kosher or sea salt
1/4 teaspoon white pepper, preferably freshly ground
Pinch of Cayenne
Pinch of ground nutmeg
1/2 cup plain dry breadcrumbs
1-1/4 pounds fresh, or good-quality frozen puff pastry, thawed
12 very fresh, thinly-sliced pompano fillets, about 2 ounces each
1-1/2 cups Green Peppercorn Sauce, warm, for serving (recipe follows)
Sprigs of fresh parsley, for garnish

Chill the bowl of a food processor in the refrigerator for 15 minutes.

Place the scallops in the processor and pulse on and off, scraping down the sides of the bowl as necessary, until they reach a mousse-like consistency. Add the carrots, celery and shallots and pulse quickly just to blend. Do not over-process. Transfer the mixture to a mixing bowl and add the cream, about one-third of the beaten eggs, the salt, white pepper, Cayenne, and nutmeg. Mix gently with a rubber spatula until only just combined, then add the breadcrumbs and fold gently together.

If necessary, roll out the puff pastry to 1/8-inch thick on a lightly floured board (frozen, supermarket puff pastry is usually pre-rolled). Using a pastry cutter in the form of a fish (ideally, 8-1/2 x 5-1/2-inches) cut twelve fish shapes from the pastry. (If you don't have a fish-shaped cutter, cut a simple fish shape out of cardboard, then use it as a guide, cutting around it with a sharp knife. Or, simply cut twelve rectangles.)

Place six of the pastry fish on a large baking sheet lined with baking parchment. Place one pompano fillet on top of each pastry fish, top the fish with one sixth of the scallop mousse and place another pompano fillet on the top.

Brush the exposed edges of the lower layer of pastry with a little of the beaten egg, then cover the second fillet with a second pastry fish. Seal the two pastry pieces together by crimping the edges with your fingers or a fork. Use small pieces of leftover pastry to form eyes, gills, scales and tail to decorate the fish-shaped shells. Chill for at least 30 minutes or up to 6 hours.

Preheat the oven to 350°. Brush the tops of each package with beaten egg.

Bake the packages for 20 to 25 minutes, or until the pastry turns golden brown. Spoon about 1/4 cup of the Green Peppercorn Sauce onto each of six dinner plates. Center a pompano croûte on the sauce, garnish with a parsley sprig and serve at once.

Green Peppercorn Sauce

YIELD: **2** CUPS

2 tablespoons unsalted butter
1 large shallot, finely chopped
1/2 cup dry white wine
2 cups fish stock, homemade or from a good quality supplier (see page 204)
1 clove garlic, very finely chopped
1 bouquet garni (see page 217)
1 tablespoon dried green peppercorns
1-1/2 tablespoons cornstarch
Kosher or sea salt
6 green onions, white and light green parts only, finely chopped
1/2 cup heavy cream

In a large saucepan, melt the butter over medium heat. Add the shallot and cook, stirring, until translucent about 3 minutes. Add the white wine, fish stock, garlic and bouquet garni. Increase the heat so the sauce simmers and reduce the liquid to about one-third of its volume (this will take about 8 minutes).

Add the green peppercorns, lower the heat to low and simmer gently for 10 minutes more. In a small bowl, stir the cornstarch into 1 tablespoon of water. Stir 1 tablespoon of the hot sauce into the cornstarch mixture, then return the cornstarch mixture to the pan and simmer gently for about 2 minutes, until the sauce will nicely coat a spoon.

Season to taste with salt, then stir in the green onions and cream. Bring to a simmer and cook for 5 minutes, just to thicken slightly. Remove the bouquet garni before serving.

The sauce may be made up to 2 days ahead of time. Cover and refrigerate, then reheat over very low heat, stirring occasionally. If the sauce gets too thick after refrigeration, stir in 1/2 teaspoon of water to loosen.

The Count's Ballroom

The Count's Ballroom seats 200 and is a popular venue for evenings of dinner and dancing as well as receptions, weddings, rehearsal dinners and debutante galas.

The ballroom when Casbarian acquired Arnaud's.

Weddings

Many vows have been exchanged at Arnaud's, whether they were toasted at an engagement party, rehearsal dinner or afterward in a grand reception or simple dinner for two.

When the Casbarians hosted the rehearsal dinner for Archie, Jr. and his fiancée Adrienne Grognet, it was an occasion when Arnaud's sparkled and glowed its brightest.

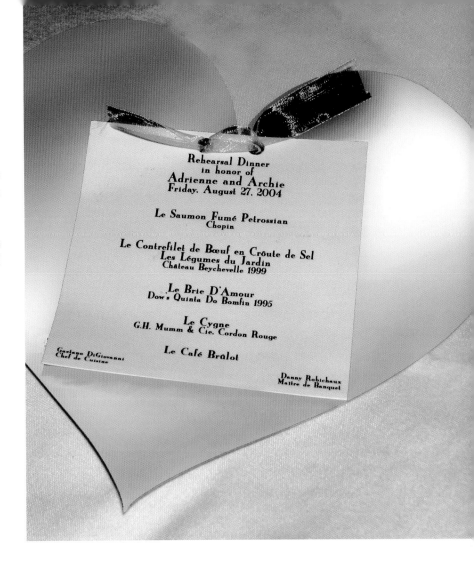

Smoked Salmon Rosettes

An engaging appetizer: smoked salmon of the finest available quality is sliced into 1-inch strips, then rolled gently into a rosette shape. These are served simply, crowned with a dollop of crème fraiche and capers.

Bread is cut into heart shapes, then toasted lightly in the oven.

Festive Ice Bucket

Waiters pour vodka from a frozen ice bucket into each guest's glass, beginning an evening of toasts. Vodka, with its high alcohol content, does not freeze.

For really striking frozen bottles, sink them into a water-filled milk carton or other container larger than the bottle with an inch or two of clearance all the way around it. Carefully place flowers under water around the bottle and freeze overnight. Hold the frozen carton under hot water for a few seconds to loosen it and slip the ice and bottle out of the container. Wrap the bottom of the ice bucket in a linen towel and pour into individual glasses.

Boeuf en Croûte de Sel

Serves 15 to 18

FOR THE CRUST:
4 pounds all-purpose flour
2 teaspoons finely chopped fresh rosemary
2 teaspoons finely chopped fresh thyme
2/3 cup chopped fresh parsley
2 tablespoons granulated garlic
2 teaspoons coarsely cracked black pepper
4 cups egg whites (from about 3 dozen eggs)
1 pound rock salt

1 whole sirloin strip, about 11 pounds, almost all fat trimmed away
1/2 cup olive oil
3 tablespoons Kosher or sea salt
3 tablespoons coarsely cracked black pepper
About 2 cups all-purpose flour (for rolling out the dough)
3 large eggs, for the egg wash
1/4 cup water, for the egg wash

Ideally, use a heavy-duty mixer for this recipe. If the mixer overheats, turn it off and allow the motor to cool before continuing.

In the bowl of a large standing mixer fitted with the dough hook, combine the flour, rosemary, thyme, parsley, garlic and pepper. Stir with a fork and let rest for about 20 minutes to allow the flour to absorb the flavors.

Add the egg whites to the flour mixture and mix at low speed for 3 to 5 minutes, until thoroughly combined. Add the rock salt and mix for 2 to 3 minutes more. The dough will be quite thick and should be very elastic. Cover the bowl with plastic wrap and refrigerate for one hour before using.

Brush the trimmed sirloin strip on all sides with olive oil and sprinkle generously with salt and pepper. Place a large, heavy roasting or braising pan over high heat and when it is very hot, sear the sirloin on all four sides, searing for about 3 minutes per side. With tongs, transfer the sirloin to a rack to cool while you roll out the dough.

Preheat oven to 450°.

On a lightly floured surface roll out the dough into a large rectangle about 3/4 inches thick and 2 inches longer than the sirloin.

Lay the sirloin lengthwise, fat-side down, in the center of the dough rectangle with 1 inch of dough extending at each end of the meat. Fold the dough over the sirloin to completely cover and seal the meat inside, trimming excess dough as you go and making sure the edges and corners are tightly sealed by pinching hard with your fingers. Gently transfer to a large baking sheet lined with parchment paper. Whisk together the eggs and water thoroughly and brush the entire exposed surface of the dough with the egg wash.

Bake for 35 minutes, then rotate the pan one-half turn and bake for approximately 35 minutes more. (For medium to medium-rare, remove the roast from the oven when the internal temperature reaches 120°) Let stand for 15 minutes, then slice carefully and serve

TIP: Use heavy-duty tongs, rather than a roasting fork, to turn the meat as you sear it, otherwise the juices will run out.

Brie en Croûte

SERVES 4

Cheese is enjoying renewed popularity as a course at the dinner table; it is generally served prior to dessert. Casbarian is a fan of en Croûte, or wrapped, presentations and the Brie did not escape his attention.

Brie en Croûte is often combined with nuts and various fruits in its flaky pastry package. When serving a large group, it is advisable to avoid hidden nuts in dishes. They may trigger a reaction by those who are allergic to them.

Arnaud's created heart-shaped Brie en Croûte for Archie, Jr. and Adrienne's rehearsal dinner, but almost any shape can be cut out. Make a cardboard template to follow, with the top one a duplicate, 1/2-inch larger all the way around to accommodate the drape over the cheese.

2 sheets packaged frozen puff pastry, thawed for 15 to 20 minutes
1 tablespoon unsalted butter
1/2 cup walnut pieces (optional)
8 ounce wheel of ripe Brie cheese
1/4 cup brown sugar
1 large egg, beaten

Preheat the oven to 375°. Unfold the puff pastry and place on a lightly floured surface. In a saucepan, melt the butter over medium-low heat. Add the walnuts and sauté until golden brown, about 5 minutes. Set aside. Cut the cheese into four equal, pie-shaped wedges. Cut each sheet of puff pastry into four 4-inch squares.

Center a piece of cheese on each 4-inch square and place the walnuts on top. Sprinkle the brown sugar over the mixture. Top each wedge of cheese with another pastry square, draping it gently over the top. Press the top and bottom edges together firmly to create a package and place on a rimmed baking sheet.

Brush the beaten egg over top and sides of each package. Bake for 20 minutes, until the pastry is golden brown. Serve with croutons or lightly toasted bread, which may also be cut into fanciful shapes.

Basic Sorbet

Sorbet is a wonderfully versatile treat. It may make an appearance between courses as a savory of citrus juices or herbal essences such as basil or rosemary. It is more often flavored with fruit juices as a dessert. (A sorbet can also give the cook an extra few minutes to complete preparation of the next dish.)

Granita, similar to sorbet, is a frozen chunk of flavored ice which is quickly scraped with a spoon. The resulting shaved crystals are served in the same manner as sorbet.

To create your own ice sculptures in various shapes, use special molds which are available at most gourmet kitchen stores.

Accompany sorbet or granita with fancy cookies or candies when serving as dessert.

Frozen swans cradling blood orange sorbet glow from the tiny lights placed underneath the sculpted ice. When they were presented at the rehearsal dinner, the room's lights were lowered and the illusion created wedges of swans swimming through the night as the waiters raised and lowered their trays.

Blood Orange Sorbet

YIELD: 1 QUART

(Any fresh citrus fruit may be substituted)

2-1/2 cups water
1 cup granulated sugar
Zest of 2 scrubbed blood oranges, removed in strips
2-2/3 cups fresh blood orange juice
1/3 cup fresh lemon juice

Combine the water and sugar in a saucepan; bring to a boil, stirring. Add the orange zest and reduce the heat. Simmer for 5 minutes, then remove from the heat. Pour the mixture through a wire mesh strainer, discard the orange zest and cool completely to room temperature.

Place the mixture in the container of an automatic ice-cream maker and freeze for 20 to 30 minutes, until you have a thick, thoroughly frozen slurry. Pack the sorbet into a plastic container and place in the freezer until frozen hard.

Raspberry Sorbet

YIELD: 1 PINT

If you use a blender to make this mixture, be sure to purée in small amounts so it will get really smooth.

10 ounce package frozen raspberries
1/4 cup granulated sugar
1/4 cup fresh orange juice
1 tablespoon fresh lemon juice
1 tablespoon Grand Marnier, or other orange-flavored liqueur

In the bowl of a food processor fitted with the metal blade, combine all the ingredients. Purée until completely smooth, then place the mixture in the container of an ice-cream machine and freeze for 20 to 30 minutes, until you have a thick, thoroughly frozen slurry. Pack the sorbet into a plastic container and place in freezer until frozen hard.

Easy Elegance

Dinner parties are a big part of the delight Orleanians take in eating well. The pleasure begins with the process of choosing a theme to anchor the evening, drawing up a guest list, seating everyone, designing the menu and selecting wines, flowers and small favors.

Jane Casbarian is an expert at planning and executing special evenings. Her wicked sense of humor seasons these occasions and one favorite ploy is to rotate guests around the tables.

Guests are initially seated with place cards, then, at the conclusion of each course, ladies move two places to their left. The gentlemen get to charm a different lady at each turn and no one ever lacks for conversation.

Birthdays, Halloween, political events, holidays and family occasions are all great reasons for a party.

The table settings are always spectacular, and are punctuated with unexpected props relating to the theme.

New Orleans' Bourbon Street becomes one more reason to dress up on each All Hallow's Eve. Costume is *de rigueur* for guests, and regular attendees are expected to change their fancy dress ideas each year.

Left to right. Jane's sister, Vickie Moat (Marilyn Monroe); Jane (Dorothy) and Archie Casbarian (the Straw Man); Billy (as an incarcerated judge) and Kit Wohl (Lady Justice) participate in the ritual costuming.

Mardi Gras and the Gold Room go together like Carnival's colors of purple, green and gold. For this cheerful purpose, purple represents justice; green, faith; gold, power.

The richness of the room's décor lends itself to glorious occasions and festivities. The Gold Room was also Germaine's favorite place for glittering events.

The corner cabinets showcase elaborate Mardi Gras invitations and memorabilia. Up to 40 seated guests can be accommodated in the Gold Room.

Germaine was regal in the shimmering gold lamé gown she wore as Queen of Naiads for the official opening of the museum and a gala Carnival Ball on September 15, 1983. On Casbarian's arm, she was escorted among her subjects, acknowledging them with a nod of her crowned head and a wave of her scepter as they slowly circled the Count's Ballroom. Later that evening, in the Gold Room, the Casbarians hosted a Queen's Supper in her honor.

Mardi Gras

For Mardi Gras, each *bal masque* requires a splendid gown or costume to carry out the theme of the tableau. For the Krewe of Sparta in 1954, the theme was "Royal Repast." Germaine ruled as "Vintage Champagne," with attendants dressed as "Creole Gumbo," "Sizzling Steaks" and other dishes. Many of the gowns were made in Europe and the amount of intricate detail was quite astonishing. Today, almost all of these formal, elaborate gowns are made in New Orleans.

The Casbarians paid tribute to Germaine Wells by creating a Mardi Gras museum in her honor on the second floor of the restaurant. Named the "Queen's Collection," the display features thirteen of Germaine's costumes along with gowns worn by her mother and daughter, four King's costumes worn by the Count, and six children's costumes. It is considered bad luck to wear a Queen's gown twice, so Germaine had a duplicate of her gold creation made to be worn for other occasions.

The museum houses sparkling faux jewels, Carnival invitations, masks, favors and vintage photos, providing a glimpse of the private celebration of Mardi Gras that is rarely seen by anyone outside New Orleans.

Just three months after the gala museum opening, on December 15, 1983, Germaine Cazenave Wells died in her father's mansion on Esplanade Avenue. At her request, she was buried in the golden gown, and the funeral cortege taking her to her final resting place at Metairie Cemetery passed by the restaurant one last time.

Germaine's love of theatre also found expression in the celebration of Mardi Gras. She ruled over 22 Carnival balls, more than any other person in New Orleans, starting in 1937 with the Krewe of Iris. Germaine said that her favorite ball was in 1938 when she reigned as queen of Prometheus and her father was king.

Rock Cornish Game Hens Twelfth Night

Carnival commences on Twelfth Night (January 6), which ushers in a hectic social season of parties, balls and parades. Several weeks later, the season culminates on Mardi Gras (Fat Tuesday). For many families, getting into the swing of the season starts with Twelfth Night Supper at Arnaud's, a tradition revelers have enjoyed since the early days of the restaurant.

Germaine celebrated by introducing Rock Cornish Game Hen Twelfth Night, a very old-fashioned, rich dish which is still served at Arnaud's but only on January 6. She adored her father and emulated him in many ways, including the creation of recipes.

This dish is complex, but like Mardi Gras and Carnival, it's all worth it in the end. To break up the preparation over two days, prepare and refrigerate the Bordelaise Sauce and the stuffing a day in advance. If you choose this method, additional time in the oven will be required.

FOR THE STUFFING:
2 ounces pork tenderloin, cut into 1/2-inch cubes
8 ounces veal top round, cut into 1/2-inch cubes
1 ounce fatback or salt pork, cut into 1/2-inch cubes
2 shallots, finely chopped
2 large eggs, lightly beaten
2 to 4 tablespoons heavy cream
1/2 cup ruby port
1 tablespoon chopped flat-leaf parsley
1/2 teaspoon fresh thyme leaves
Kosher or sea salt and freshly ground pepper

4 Rock Cornish game hens, about 8 ounces each
4 slices bacon
1 quart Veal Stock (see page 205)
2 tablespoons clarified butter (see page 206)
8 ounces white mushrooms, quartered
1 tomato, peeled, seeded and chopped (or 1/2 cup canned diced tomato)
1 cup Bordelaise Sauce (see page 207)
Kosher or sea salt and white pepper, preferably freshly ground
1 tablespoon chopped flat-leaf parsley
Cherry tomatoes and sprigs of flat-leaf or curly parsley for garnish

First, make the stuffing: Chill the cubes of meat and fatback for 30 minutes. Place in a food processor and pulse into a smooth paste. Transfer to a large bowl and add the shallots, egg, 2 tablespoons of the cream, the port, parsley and thyme. With a fork, blend until all the ingredients are evenly distributed. (The mixture should be very moist, but not loose; two more tablespoons of cream may be added if necessary.) Season generously with salt and pepper. If desired, cover and refrigerate for up to 24 hours before stuffing.

Preheat the oven to 400°.

Season the birds inside and out with salt and pepper and stuff loosely with the stuffing mixture. Wrap a slice of bacon around each bird, wrapping across the opening to hold the stuffing in. Secure the bacon with toothpicks.

Place the hens in a roasting pan and pour the veal stock over and around them. Cover the pan with aluminum foil and braise in the oven for 45 to 60 minutes, until tender and the juices at the thigh joint run clear when pierced with a small, sharp knife. (If the birds were prepared and stuffed the night before, use the longer cooking time.)

While the birds are braising, place a saucepan over medium-high heat and add the clarified butter. When it is hot, add and sauté the mushrooms for about 5 minutes, until tender. Stir in the chopped tomatoes and Bordelaise Sauce and season to taste with salt and pepper. Heat through, stirring, then stir in the parsley and remove from the heat.

When the birds are done, transfer them to a warm platter, discarding the bacon. Garnish the edges of the platter with cherry tomatoes and parsley sprigs and re-warm the sauce, if necessary. Drizzle the sauce over the hens and serve immediately.

Pineapple and Louisiana Yams à la Germaine

SERVES 12

6 yams (or sweet potatoes)
12 pineapple slices (canned)
2/3 cup all-purpose flour
1/3 cup whole milk
1/2 cup unsalted butter
12 maraschino cherries
1/2 cup brown sugar
1/2 cup rum
2 tablespoons sherry

Boil yams until tender. Peel and cut in half. Roll the pineapple slices and yams in flour, then in milk and again in flour.

In a large skillet over medium-high heat, fry the pineapple slices and then the yams until golden brown. Preheat the oven to 400°.

Butter a large baking pan. Arrange the yams in the pan and top each half with a slice of pineapple. Place a cherry in the center of each slice. Sprinkle with the brown sugar. Place in the oven and bake for 5 minutes.

Heat the rum and pour over the hot yams. Ignite with a long match. When the flames die out, transfer to a heated serving platter and drizzle with the sherry. Serve immediately.

Watercress à la Germaine

SERVES 6

3 bunches watercress, cleaned and trimmed
2 cups sliced mushrooms
12 cherry tomatoes
Watercress dressing (recipe below)

Divide the watercress among six salad plates, top each with sliced mushrooms and add dressing. Garnish each plate with 2 cherry tomatoes.

Watercress Dressing

YIELD: 1 CUP

1/2 cup mayonnaise
1/4 cup sour cream
1/8 cup Creole cream cheese (see page 101)
3/4 teaspoon crushed green peppercorns
2 tablespoons chopped green onions or scallions
1/4 teaspoon Worcestershire sauce
1/8 teaspoon Tabasco Sauce
Kosher or sea salt and white pepper, preferably freshly ground

Using a mixer at low speed, blend the mayonnaise, sour cream and cream cheese for 3 minutes. Add the remaining ingredients and blend for 3 minutes more. Season to taste with salt and white pepper

Note: Creole cream cheese is a New Orleans original. It is a single large curd surrounded by cream. To substitute, pour heavy cream over either farmer cheese or large-curd cottage cheese.

Celebration on the Half Shell

Briny, plump oysters, so fresh you can smell the Gulf breeze, are one of New Orleans' favorite stages for culinary creativity. They might be served with the iridescent shell open, glistening on a bed of crushed ice, or starring in a favorite recipe.

Aficionados gather at fine restaurants such as Arnaud's, where a dozen bi-valves are served in style, or at oyster bars such as Arnaud's casual Creole café, Remoulade, where they often elbow into a choice spot in front of the oyster shucker.

Cocktail sauce is mixed according to individual whim from condiments placed on the bar, along with saltine crackers. Keeping up with the shucker is a matter of pride, and the final mound of shells lays testament to the experience.

At home, families and friends will often purchase a burlap sack of fresh oysters and enjoy them on the half shell as soon as they are opened, bake them in the oven with sauces or toppings, create soups and gumbos, seafood gratins or grill them on the barbecue. It is an all-day, al fresco affair.

Oysters Arnaud

Oysters Arnaud includes five different recipes for baked toppings. They are Oysters Bienville, Oysters Rockefeller, Oysters Kathryn, Oysters Ohan and Oysters Suzette. Oysters Kathryn was created and named for Casbarian's daughter, Katy, and Oysters Ohan was similarly devised in honor of the late Ohan Casbarian, beloved patriarch of the Casbarian family and Katy's grandfather. Each recipe is included here; however preparing them all at once may be a daunting task. Presentation of just one recipe is still a singular pleasure and easier on the cook.

The toppings may be made a day in advance and refrigerated, then used to crown the waiting oysters before baking them together and serving immediately.

"How ya like dem ersters?" asked New Orleans Mayor Robert Maestri as he and President Franklin Roosevelt dined on Oysters Rockefeller.

In the 1930s and '40s, Arnaud's was already established as the city's trend-setter. Photo courtesy of the Historic New Orleans Collection.

Oysters Bienville

SERVES 8 TO 10

Arnaud's original Oysters Bienville takes its name from the restaurant's location at 813 Rue Bienville, which in turn was named for the founder of New Orleans, Jean Baptiste le Moyne, Sieur de Bienville, governor of the original French Colony. As the story goes, the Count created Oysters Bienville as a competitive response to the great attention Oysters Rockefeller was attracting at Antoine's, so named in honor of John D. Rockefeller.

1 tablespoon vegetable oil
2/3 cup finely chopped white mushrooms
4 tablespoons (2 ounces, 1/2 stick) unsalted butter
1-1/2 teaspoons very finely chopped garlic
4 large shallots, finely chopped
1/2 pound cooked shrimp, finely diced
1 tablespoon all-purpose flour
1/2 cup brandy
1/2 cup heavy cream
1 teaspoon ground white pepper
6 tablespoons grated Romano cheese
4 tablespoons dry breadcrumbs
1/4 cup finely chopped flat-leaf parsley
1 teaspoon Kosher or sea salt
Freshly ground black pepper
1/2 teaspoon Cayenne pepper
2 dozen plump, salty, oysters, freshly shucked and the flat sides of the shells reserved
   (Note: For these baked oyster dishes, fat, briny oysters about the size of a fifty-cent
   piece are perfect.)
About 2 pounds rock salt (optional)
Lemon wedges wrapped in muslin sleeves, for serving

In a large, heavy saucepan, warm the vegetable oil and sauté the chopped mushrooms for about 4 minutes, stirring. Remove from the pan with a slotted spoon, press with another spoon to remove excess liquid and set aside.

In the same pan, melt the butter over low heat and sauté the garlic and shallots for about three minutes, stirring frequently, until softened.

Add the diced shrimp and stir to mix, then sprinkle evenly with the flour. Stir together, add the reserved mushrooms and increase heat to medium.

Stirring constantly, deglaze the pan with the brandy. Stir in the cream

After years of polite sniping amongst New Orleans restaurants, Antoine's 1986 cookbook acknowledged that Arnaud's had indeed provided Oysters Bienville to the culinary world. Meanwhile, both signature dishes are happily served at restaurants across the city and around the country.

and cook for two to three minutes, until smooth. Stir in the Romano, dry breadcrumbs, parsley, salt, a touch of black pepper and the Cayenne to a soft, moundable consistency. A small amount of milk may be added if the mixture is too thick.

Remove the pan from the heat and transfer the mixture to a glass or ceramic bowl. Cool to room temperature, then refrigerate for about 1 1/2 hours, or until thoroughly chilled.

Preheat the oven to 400°. Wash the oyster shells well and pat dry. Drain the oysters and place one in each of the 24 shells, or use two smaller oysters per shell if necessary.

Place the shells in a large, heavy roasting pan lined with a 1/2-inch layer of rock salt, or place six filled oyster shells in each of four pie pans lined with salt (the salt keeps the shells upright during cooking and stops the delicious juices from escaping).

Top each oyster with one generous tablespoon of the Bienville mix and bake for 15 to 18 minutes, or until nicely browned.

The shells will be extremely hot. Carefully place 6 oysters on each hot dinner plate. If baked in pie pans of rock salt, place each pan on a dinner plate.

Garnish with a wrapped lemon wedge and serve immediately.

Oysters Rockefeller

SERVES 6

2 tablespoons unsalted butter
12 slices raw bacon, very finely chopped
4 cups finely chopped celery
1 cup seeded and de-ribbed green pepper, finely chopped
3 tablespoons very finely chopped garlic
1 cup finely chopped white onion
4 cups blanched and drained spinach, chopped (two 10 ounce packages of completely
    thawed frozen spinach may be substituted)
2 bay leaves
1 pinch dried thyme
1 pinch Cayenne pepper
2 tablespoons finely chopped flat-leaf parsley
1/3 cup Herbsaint liqueur or Pernod
1 tablespoon finely chopped fresh basil
Kosher or sea salt and freshly ground black pepper
3 dozen plump, salty oysters, freshly shucked and the flat sides of the shells reserved
About 2 pounds rock salt (optional)
Lemon wedges wrapped in muslin sleeves, for serving

In a medium sauté pan, melt the butter over medium heat and cook the bacon until the fat has been rendered and bacon is crisp, about 5 minutes.

Add the celery, green pepper, garlic and onion, then stir and sauté until the vegetables are softened, 4 to 5 minutes. Add the spinach and stir for 5 minutes more. Stir in the bay leaves, thyme, Cayenne and parsley, then drizzle in the Herbsaint and continue cooking for 1 minute, then reduce the heat and simmer for 2 minutes. Remove the bay leaves, add the basil and season to taste with salt and pepper.

In a blender or food processor, purée about half of the mixture, then stir it back into the original pan, mixing together thoroughly. Transfer to a covered container, cool to room temperature and refrigerate for about 1 hour to firm the mixture.

Preheat the oven to 400°.

Antoine's has never divulged their recipe for Oysters Rockefeller just as Arnaud's keeps their Arnaud's Sauce and Creole mustard recipes a secret. This version is very close. Antoine's insists that there is no spinach in their preparation, although most other Oysters Rockefeller recipes call for it. Attempts to duplicate the recipe without using spinach make use of parsley, shallots, celery tops or a combination of green vegetables.

Wash the flat oyster shells well, and pat them dry. Drain the oysters and place one in each prepared shell. Place the shells in a large, heavy roasting pan lined with a 1/2-inch layer of rock salt, or place six oyster shells in each of six pie pans lined with salt (the salt keeps the shells upright during cooking and stops the delicious juices from escaping).

Top each oyster with one generous tablespoon of Rockefeller sauce and bake for 15 to 18 minutes, until nicely browned.

The shells will be extremely hot. Carefully place 6 oysters on each hot dinner plate. If baked in pie pans of rock salt, place each pan on a dinner plate.

Garnish with a wrapped lemon wedge and serve immediately.

Oysters Kathryn

Serves 6

1 (7.8 ounce) can artichoke hearts, drained and finely chopped
1/2 cup fresh breadcrumbs
1 large egg, lightly beaten
1/2 cup heavy cream
1/2 teaspoon finely chopped fresh basil
1/2 cup grated Parmesan cheese
Juice of 1 lemon
1 clove garlic, very finely chopped
Kosher or sea salt and freshly ground black pepper
6 lemon wedges wrapped in muslin sleeves, for serving
3 dozen plump, salty oysters, preferably freshly shucked (in any event, you will need the flat sides of the shells for serving)
6 pans rock salt (optional)

In a mixing bowl, combine the chopped artichoke hearts, breadcrumbs, egg, cream, basil, Parmesan, lemon juice and garlic. Season to taste with salt and pepper and combine thoroughly, using a fork.

Cover and refrigerate for at least half an hour and up to 2 hours. Preheat the oven to 400°. Scrub the oyster shells well and pat them dry. Drain the oysters and place one in each shell. Place the shells on a large, heavy roasting pan (or place six oysters in each pan of rock salt). Top each oyster with a generous tablespoon of the topping mixture, smoothing it into a mound. Bake for 15 to 18 minutes, until the tops are nicely browned.

The shells will be extremely hot. Carefully place 6 oysters on each hot dinner plate (or, if baked in pans of rock salt, place each pan on a dinner plate). Garnish with a wrapped lemon wedge and serve.

Katy's signature recipe, Oysters Kathryn, was created in 1979 for her father's inaugural menu. Here, Katy and staff members conduct a review of wines offered for the restaurant's consideration.

Oysters Suzette

1/2 pound raw bacon, minced
2 green bell peppers, seeded and finely chopped
1 medium white onion, minced
2 celery stalks, strings removed, finely chopped
1/4 cup (2 ounces) pimiento, finely chopped
1/2 cup fish stock (see page 204) or oyster liquor
1 tablespoon lemon juice
1 dash Angostura bitters
1/8 teaspoon dried thyme leaves
2 tablespoons butter
2 tablespoons all-purpose flour
About 2 pounds rock salt (optional)
3 dozen plump, salty oysters, freshly shucked and the flat sides of the shells reserved
Lemon wedges or halves, wrapped in muslin sleeves, for serving

Cut lemons wrapped in a square of muslin then tied with a colorful ribbon keeps seeds from scattering when the lemon is squeezed.

In a large, heavy skillet, sauté the bacon with the green peppers, onion and celery. Stir and cook for 5 to 7 minutes until the bacon fat is rendered and the vegetables are soft. Pour off the fat.

Add the pimiento, fish stock or oyster liquor, lemon juice, bitters and thyme. Bring to a boil and cook for 5 minutes.

Meanwhile, in a separate small saucepan prepare the Roux (see page 216) by cooking the butter and flour together for 5 minutes, stirring occasionally to ensure even cooking. Blend the Roux with the vegetable mixture and stir until thickened.

Transfer the cooked mixture to a glass or ceramic bowl. Cool to room temperature, then refrigerate for about 1-1/2 hours, or until thoroughly chilled.

Preheat the oven to 400°.

Wash the oyster shells well and pat dry. Drain the oysters and place one in each of the 36 shells, or use two smaller oysters per shell if necessary.

Place the shells in a large, heavy roasting pan lined with a 1/2-inch layer of rock salt, or place six filled oyster shells in each of four pie pans lined with salt (the salt keeps the shells upright during cooking and stops the delicious juices from escaping). Top each oyster with 1 generous tablespoon of the Suzette mix and bake for 15 minutes.

The shells will be extremely hot. Carefully place 6 oysters on each hot dinner plate. If baked in pie pans of rock salt, place each pan on a dinner plate.

Garnish with a wrapped lemon wedge or halves and serve immediately.

Oysters Ohan

Serves 6

The late Ohan Casbarian raised his three sons in Beruit and Alexandria, Egypt and sent them to American universities. Ohan and his wife, Ellen, emigrated to New Orleans where they received their citizenship shortly before their eldest son, Archie, acquired Arnaud's. The restaurant was a family affair from day one, as Ohan negotiated fiercely with purveyors, placed the food orders and personally checked deliveries at the back door.

2 medium eggplants
1 cup olive oil
1/2 pound andouille or other smoked sausage,
     finely chopped
1/2 shallot, very finely chopped
1/2 yellow bell pepper, seeded, de-ribbed and
     finely chopped
1/2 medium red onion, finely chopped
2 stalks celery, finely chopped
1 small clove garlic, very finely chopped
1/4 cup white wine
1/2 cup chicken stock (see page 204) or use store-bought
2 bay leaves
Pinch of Cayenne pepper
1/2 teaspoon ground white pepper
1/2 teaspoon dried thyme
1/2 teaspoon dried marjoram
1/2 teaspoon dried oregano
Kosher or sea salt and freshly ground black pepper
3 dozen plump, salty oysters, freshly shucked and the flat sides of the shells reserved
About 2 pounds rock salt (optional)
Lemon wedges or halves wrapped in muslin sleeves, for serving

Using a nice sharp vegetable peeler, peel the eggplants, scoop out any seeds and chop finely. Place a large sauté pan over medium heat and add the olive oil. When it is hot, add the eggplant, andouille, shallot, yellow pepper, onion and celery. Sauté the mixture until the vegetables are softened and the onion is transparent, about 10 minutes. Add the garlic and cook for one minute more. Add the wine, chicken stock, and bay leaves and simmer the mixture until almost all the liquid has evaporated.

Stir in the Cayenne and white peppers, thyme, marjoram and oregano, and cook, stirring, for 4 minutes more. Taste and season with salt and pepper as desired. Remove the bay leaves and cool to room temperature, then refrigerate, covered, for at least 1-1/2 hours, to firm.

Preheat the oven to 400°

Scrub the oyster shells well and pat them dry. Drain the oysters and place one in each shell. Place the shells on a large, heavy roasting pan (or place six oysters in each pan of rock salt). Top each oyster with a generous tablespoon of the topping mixture, smoothing it into a mound. Bake for 15 to 18 minutes, until the tops are nicely browned.

The shells will be extremely hot. Carefully place 6 oysters on each hot dinner plate (or, if baked in pans of rock salt, place each pan on a dinner plate). Garnish with a wrapped lemon wedge and serve.

Oysters en Brochette

SERVES 6

2 cups all-purpose flour
2 cups buttermilk
1-1/2 teaspoons Kosher or sea salt
1/2 teaspoon freshly ground black pepper
Vegetable oil, for frying
4 dozen large oysters, shucked
12 slices bacon, sliced crosswise into four equal pieces
1 cup (8 ounces, 2 sticks) unsalted butter, clarified (see page 206)
Juice of 1/2 lemon
1 teaspoon Worcestershire sauce

For this dish, you will need metal or bamboo skewers about 8 inches long.

In a large, shallow bowl, combine the flour, salt and pepper and toss with a fork to blend.

Blanch the bacon for 3 minutes in boiling water to pre-cook. Drain and dry the bacon on a paper towel.

Place a large deep, skillet over medium-high heat and pour in vegetable oil to a depth of about 1 inch.

Wrap each oyster in a bacon slice.

Preheat the oven to its lowest setting and place an ovenproof platter lined with a paper towel inside. Dredge the oysters through the flour, shaking off the excess. Thread the oysters onto the skewers. Don't squash them together; space about 1/2 inch apart. Dredge in flour, dredge in buttermilk and dredge in flour again.

When the oil reaches 375°, fry the brochettes two at a time, until golden brown, about two minutes per side, turning over with long-handled tongs. Keep the finished brochettes warm in the oven while you fry the remaining brochettes.

To make the Lemon Butter Sauce, warm the clarified butter in a small saucepan over medium heat. Stir in the lemon juice and the Worcestershire sauce, stirring until incorporated. Drizzle a pool of warm butter sauce onto each plate and place a brochette on the top. Diners use their forks to slide the oysters and bacon off the skewers.

Oysters on the Half Shell

SERVES 6

If you plan to open your own oysters, practice before it is time to do the deed for guests. If you don't know what you're doing, the process can be time-consuming and dangerous. Special oyster knives and safety gloves are a necessity. For parties, Orleanians hire an oyster shucker to perform this feat for guests.

Many seafood restaurants have a staff member who would be happy for a little free-lance work either as an instructor or as your official party shucker. Otherwise, arrange to pick up several trays of iced and just opened oysters on the half shell from a restaurant.

A closed oyster has a muscular hinge that keeps the shells tightly closed together. Wearing the safety glove on the hand holding the oyster, nudge the knifepoint under the shell just before the hinged part and poke around until a small gap is felt. Insert the tip of the blade. Push the knife in a little further. Twist the blade firmly and pry open the oyster. Cut the attachment and discard the top shell. Cut the muscle fiber under the oyster that holds it to the shell so the oyster may be picked up with a cocktail fork or slurped in style straight from nature's little dish.

3 dozen freshly shucked oysters on the half shell
6 lemon wedges wrapped in muslin sleeves, for serving
Sprigs of flat-leaf parsley, for serving
Mignonette or Cocktail sauce (at right), for serving

Fill six shallow soup bowls with crushed ice. Nestle a small cup or ramekin into the ice in the center to hold the sauce and arrange six oysters on their half-shells around the sauce. Place each bowl of oysters on a large dinner plate. Garnish with a wrapped lemon and a sprig of parsley and serve immediately.

Mignonette Sauce

YIELD: 1-1/3 CUPS

1 cup best-quality red wine vinegar
1/2 cup very finely chopped shallots
1/2 teaspoon coarsely ground black pepper
Dash of Kosher or sea salt

Mix together in a bowl and chill until serving time.

Cocktail Sauce

YIELD: 1-1/3 CUPS

1 cup ketchup
1/4 cup prepared horseradish
1 tablespoon fresh lemon juice
1 teaspoon Worcestershire sauce
Dash of Tabasco Sauce (optional)

Mix together in a bowl and chill until serving time.

Hors d'Oeuvres, Canapes and Appetizers

Storyville was New Orleans' legal red-light district until the U.S. Navy attempted to squelch prostitution by declaring it illegal in 1917. The resourceful madams merely moved their businesses a few blocks over toward the Mississippi River, into the French Quarter. A haven for high jinks and low life, it was a tawdry, rollicking place, far from uptown residential neighborhoods. The Creole Cottage at Arnaud's was not only a former opium den but also a house of ill-repute.

The *Daily States* of September 17, 1885 published an account of a police raid at the address, identifying it as an opium den and concluding: "Just as the opium fiends were about to lock the door they were arrested."

The Creole Cottage was later to be the business place for Miss Glen Evans, an accomplished madam. She operated her discreet house next door to Arnaud's and was never raided in thirty-five years of operation, according to Christine Wiltz, author of *The Last Madam: A Life in New Orleans*.

The Creole Cottage was then acquired, and became a part of the ever-expanding restaurant. As a fine dining establishment, Arnaud's certainly served food and drink in abundance but privacy as a legacy, although not listed, was also a highlight on the menu.

In Arnaud's excellent tradition of discretion, the Creole Cottage stands alone, boasting a private street entrance which is greatly appreciated by celebrities who prefer to arrive and depart unnoticed.

The Creole Cottage at Arnaud's, 831-833 Bienville, was purchased September 19, 1946, by the Count. That transaction secured the properties down Bienville from the corner of Bourbon Street to all but one house at the end of the block.

The history of the Creole Cottage dates from May 20, 1809, when Rosetta Young, a free woman of color, inherited it from her mother. She held it until 1817 when Charles Victor Mansuy Le Pelletier purchased it. The property changed hands several times before it was sold by Mme. Marie Roi Villerie Ducourneau to Elizabeth Norwood on November 18, 1823.

Records at The Historic New Orleans Collection show that on February 23, 1883, the property was sold at auction. An advertisement for the auction in the *Courier* newspaper tempted bids with the description of "a lot of ground at the corner of Bienville and Dauphine Streets" and the house as "6 rooms 5 with fireplace, brick kitchen, servant's rooms, a shed for horse and gig, a good well and large water cask."

The ad describes another lot adjoining the first, with 42 foot front on Bienville, by 65 foot depth with buildings. "...good new Brick house, divided into four rooms, back gallery enclosed with glass doors and Venetia blinds… The house is covered with tiles and the wood work is well finished," and "a two-story brick kitchen w/servant's rooms; good well…large water cask, privies, etc."

Starters

An appetite stimulant is appreciated everywhere as the prelude to a magnificent meal. Some restaurants offer an *amuse bouche*, a tiny bite or a tease. Cocktail parties are a stage for passing canapes or hors d'oeuvres and the first course of a seated dinner is nothing but delicious anticipation of things to come. It is a small detail of a wonderful meal and an opportunity for the chef to show off in small but tasty ways.

The Creole Cottage today could be a private home with its wet bar and other facilities for special events. It seats 90 for dining and up to 120 for receptions. Part of the charm of all Arnaud's private dining rooms' decor is the extraordinary attention to detail, rarely found in a restaurant.

Pommes Soufflé

SERVES 6 TO 8

Arnaud's most dramatic appetizer is the Pommes Soufflé. These are probably the fanciest French fries you'll ever eat. We recommend making them at home only if there is absolutely no way you can get here.

One evening at the last minute, in the south of France, it is said, a cook hastily plunged already-fried potatoes into a second bath of hot oil, to bring them up to temperature. He was amazed to see the potatoes magically puff up, filling with air inside a crisp exterior. And thus was born one of Arnaud's signature dishes: Pommes Soufflé.

In Arnaud's kitchen one special chef is assigned the exacting task of preparing this perennially popular dish. It is, and appropriately so, a noble and respected position. The result: crisp pillows of golden, air-filled potato.

Mystery author Julie Smith spent several days working in Arnaud's kitchen to research how one could best dispatch a victim. She selected the vat of frying oil for Pommes Soufflés or the Buffalo chopper.

In other words, beware: exercise caution when frying at home. Hot oil is dangerous!

2 large Idaho or Russet potatoes (about 12 ounces each), not too old or too young
4 quarts vegetable oil
Kosher or sea salt
Béarnaise sauce (see page 207)

In a large, deep pot or an electric deep fryer, heat the oil to 300°.

Place a large baking sheet lined with a double layer of paper towels on the work surface.

Peel the potatoes and trim all sides to form the largest rectangles possible. Cut into 1/8-inch slices—a mandolin will do this beautifully—but in any case it is vital for the slices to be uniform. Rinse the slices thoroughly in cool water and pat dry with plenty of paper towels.

When the oil has reached the correct temperature, place about one third of the potatoes in a wire basket and submerge in the hot oil. When the potatoes float to the top, lift up the basket and allow the excess oil to drain back into the fryer. As each batch is pre-cooked, transfer to the baking sheet and then fry the remaining batches. The potatoes can stay at room temperature for up to 3 hours before you proceed to the second frying.

Just before you are ready to serve, re-heat the oil (or increase the temperature if serving right away) to the smoking point, about 450°. Return the potatoes to the fryer in batches. They should puff up immediately. Fry until golden brown, dry, and crisp. As each batch is cooked, remove from the oil and drain on paper towels. Salt lightly and serve immediately on napkin-lined plates, with Béarnaise sauce, if desired.

Note: In order to make the cuts uniform, we highly recommend the use of a mandolin, available at most good kitchen supply shops. The age of the potatoes is also very important. New potatoes have too much moisture and will not puff. Soft, old potatoes will not puff. High humidity will also cause failure. At times, Arnaud's simply cannot serve these popular potatoes due to the prevailing atmospheric conditions. No matter how hard the chef tries, they simply will not puff.

While we serve these airy puffs with Béarnaise sauce, they are perfectly delicious with no adornment whatsoever.

Escargots en Casserole

SERVES 6

At Arnaud's, escargots come to the table piping hot, individually nestled in small pots underneath a cap of puff pastry. It is a Casbarian recipe and a family favorite. This variation on the classic service eliminates the need for clamps and special forks. Ceramic snail pots are available at gourmet and restaurant supply shops. You will need 36 of them for this recipe.

36 canned snails, well rinsed and drained
1-1/8 cups Garlic Butter (see page 206), softened if necessary
3/4 pound freshly made or good-quality frozen puff pastry, thawed
1 large egg, beaten

Preheat the oven to 420°.

Place each snail in a snail pot or the tiniest possible size of ramekin (with a diameter of about 2-inches). Spread about 1/2 tablespoon of the Garlic Butter over each snail.

On a lightly floured surface, roll the puff pastry out to 1/8-inch thickness. Using a 2-inch pastry cutter, cut out 36 circles. Brush the rims of the pot or ramekin with a little water and cover each snail pot with a circle of pastry, pressing the edges lightly to make sure the pastry adheres. Brush the top of the pastry with beaten egg.

Bake for about 8 minutes, until the pastry turns golden brown and serve immediately.

ONE OF THE COUNT'S MENU NOTES FROM THE 1930S

TO OUR GUESTS

"Some of the names in this menu will probably puzzle you. They are the names of dishes belonging to what we call 'La Cuisine Classique,' as expounded by great chefs, past and present, such as Careme, Dubois, Bernard of Paris, Escoffier, Francatelli of London and Florence, Ranhoffer, Oscar, Rector of New York, and many in New Orleans too numerous to mention…we cannot simplify, alter or change them. The waiters will gladly tell you what they constitute. Everything progresses—customs and modes of living change with the passing of time. The Art of Cooking will inevitably follow the same trend. Very commendably, we do not eat half of what we ate in the past. Our tastes are becoming more and more exacting, and the chefs of tomorrow will probably, without changing the fundamental culinary principles created by the past masters, evolve an Art of Cooking more simple, more scientific, more precise, in keeping with the tendencies, changes and needs of the times. But why worry. Let us appreciate and enjoy now its subtle, savoring, satisfying goodness."

The Count's Deviled Eggs

Almost every Southern household has at least one egg platter. It is an over-sized ceramic or glass plate with 12 egg shaped indentations. When deviled (or stuffed) eggs are brought for a picnic or family party, recovery of the plate is of supreme importance. The deviled egg platter is also a popular wedding shower gift and many of these peculiar dishes are passed down from generation to generation. Deviled eggs may also be served atop a nest of colorful shredded lettuces dotted with olives.

8 extra large or jumbo hard-cooked eggs
2 tablespoons mayonnaise
1 tablespoon Arnaud's Creole Mustard
1 teaspoon red wine vinegar
About 4 cups finely shredded iceberg lettuce
1/2 cup Arnaud's Remoulade Sauce (see page 203)

Remove the shells from the eggs and cut them in half lengthwise. Carefully remove the yolks and place them in a small bowl.

Trim about 1/8-inch from the rounded side of each egg white so it will sit upright. Place the egg white halves on a platter.

To the egg yolks, add the mayonnaise, mustard and vinegar. Mash the mixture with a fork until it is well blended and slightly chunky.

Mound a generous teaspoon of the filling into the hollows of the egg whites. If desired, refrigerate for up to 4 hours before serving (cover with plastic wrap if chilling for more than 30 minutes). Fill the egg whites with the yolk mixture. Refrigerate if not serving immediately.

Spread some of the shredded lettuce on each salad plate and place two stuffed egg halves in the center. Drizzle a little Arnaud's Sauce over each egg and serve.

Artichoke en Surprise

Germaine loved surprises—in more ways than one. Hidden, or enclosed stuffings, were some of her favorites.

6 large, firm artichokes, leaves tightly clustered
    (not splayed at the flower end)
2 lemons, halved

STUFFING
1 pound lump crabmeat, picked over, or substitute
    cooked, peeled, and coarsely chopped shrimp
3/4 cup mayonnaise
2 green onions, ends trimmed and finely chopped

CHAMPAGNE VINAIGRETTE
1 large egg yolk
1 tablespoon plus 1/4 cup champagne vinegar
2 cups extra-virgin olive oil
1 shallot, finely chopped
8 leaves fresh basil, chopped
Kosher or sea salt and freshly ground black pepper

With kitchen shears, trim off the thorned ends of the artichoke leaves. Place a large vegetable steamer in a large saucepan (a bamboo steamer set over a wok works well—cover with foil if the lid will not fit over the artichokes). Add cold water to the 3-inch level in the saucepan; squeeze in the juice of the lemons and drop 1 of the lemon halves into the water. Cut off the stems of the artichokes flat against the bottom, rub the bases with another lemon half, and snuggle them side-by-side in the steamer. Bring the water to a boil over medium heat and cover the pan tightly. Reduce the heat so the water simmers gently, and steam for 45 minutes to 1 hour, until the leaves pull easily away and the artichoke meat at the ends of each leaf is tender. Place upside-down on a baking sheet lined with a doubled layer of paper towels and refrigerate for at least 2 hours and up to overnight.

To make the vinaigrette, in a mixing bowl, whisk together the egg yolk and 1 tablespoon of the vinegar until smooth. Whisking all the time, add the oil slowly in a thin stream, whisking until the vinaigrette thickens to the consistency of mustard. Whisk in the remaining vinegar, then stir in the shallot, basil, about 1/2 teaspoon of salt and pepper to taste. Cover and refrigerate for at least 1 hour to allow the flavors to blend. Taste for seasoning.

Just before serving, place the crabmeat, mayonnaise and green onions in a bowl and pour in 1 cup of the vinaigrette (reserve the remaining vinaigrette for another use). Using a fork, mix together gently, but avoid breaking up all the nice big lumps of crabmeat. Pull down the tips of the artichoke leaves and tuck as much of the stuffing mixture inside as possible. Serve immediately.

Artichoke Stuffed with Shrimp and Brie

SERVES 2

For a slightly lighter variation, omit the Brie, and instead blend together 1/4 cup grated Parmesan with 1/2 cup (4 ounces) softened cream cheese. Put a dab of the cheese mixture in each leaf section and cover the center with cheese mix before broiling.

2 medium, firm artichokes, leaves tightly clustered
    (not splayed at the flower end)
1 lemon, halved

FOR THE STUFFING:
1 small onion, finely chopped
2 cloves garlic, very finely chopped
1/3 cup seeded, de-ribbed and finely chopped red bell pepper
6 green onions, green parts only, finely chopped
1/2 cup finely chopped flat-leaf parsley
1 teaspoon finely chopped fresh thyme leaves
1 cup cooked bay shrimp, chopped
1 cup fresh bread crumbs
1/2 cup white wine
2 tablespoons fresh lemon juice
1/3 cup grated Parmesan cheese
1/4 teaspoon Cayenne pepper
1/4 teaspoon freshly ground black pepper
1 teaspoon Creole Seasoning (see page 218 or use store-bought)
4 ounces Brie (not too soft), cut into 1/4 inch cubes

With kitchen shears, trim off the thorned ends of the artichoke leaves. Place a vegetable steamer in a large saucepan. Add cold water to the 3-inch level in the saucepan, squeeze in the juice of half the lemon and drop the lemon half into the water. Cut off the stems of the artichokes flat against the bottom, rub the bases with the remaining lemon half and place them base-down in the steamer. Bring the water to a boil over medium heat and cover the pan tightly. Reduce the heat so the water simmers gently, and steam for 35 to 45 minutes, until the leaves pull easily away and the artichoke meat at the ends of each leaf is tender. Place upside-down on a baking sheet lined with a doubled layer of paper towels and refrigerate for at least 2 hours and up to overnight if desired.

Place a skillet over medium-low heat and add the olive oil. Add the onion, garlic and red pepper and sauté until tender but not brown, 10 minutes. Stir in the green onions, parsley and thyme. Add the shrimp, breadcrumbs, white wine and lemon juice and stir well. Remove from the heat and add the Parmesan, Cayenne and Cajun Seasoning. Combine thoroughly and taste for seasoning.

Open out the outer leaves of each artichoke a little to expose the inner, pale leaves. Pull out and discard the centers of each one, exposing the fuzzy, indigestible chokes. Scrape out the chokes carefully with a small spoon, carefully keeping all the outer leaves in place.

Ease outward each of the remaining leaves and stuff a teaspoon of shrimp mixture into each section, going around the artichoke. Fill the centers loosely with more stuffing.

Preheat the broiler to high heat.

Place a cube of Brie on top of the filling in each section and cover the center filling with several cubes of Brie. Place the artichokes on a baking sheet and set under the hot broiler, watching carefully so they don't burn. Broil until the cheese is melted and bubbly and serve at once.

Crawfish Beignets

YIELD: 60 APPETIZERS OR BITES

Beignets (say ben-yea) *are usually a sweet fried donut served with café au lait. Here, they are treated as a savory stuffed with seafood. The number of variations are as endless as your imagination. Substitute crabmeat, shrimp cheese or any savory filling for the crawfish, if desired.*

1-1/2 cups all-purpose flour
1-1/2 tablespoons baking powder
1/2 teaspoon fresh thyme leaves
1 clove garlic, very finely chopped
1 teaspoon Kosher or sea salt
2 large eggs
1/2 cup whole milk
1/2 teaspoon Cayenne pepper
1 pound cleaned crawfish tails, chopped
1 roasted sweet red pepper, drained and finely chopped
1 green onion, white and light green parts, finely chopped
1 tablespoon finely chopped flat-leaf chopped parsley
Shortening, for deep frying
Mango-Ginger Chutney (see page 214)

In large bowl, mix together the flour, baking powder, thyme, garlic and salt. In another bowl, beat the eggs and milk together and stir in the Cayenne pepper. Drizzle the egg mixture into the dry ingredients, whisking all the time until smooth. Fold in the crawfish, red pepper, green onion and parsley.

Half fill a deep, heavy pot or an electric deep fryer with shortening and heat to 375°.

Place a baking sheet lined with a double layer of paper towels in the oven and heat to its lowest setting.

Drop batter, a tablespoon at a time, into the hot oil. Fry four or five beignets, without crowding, until golden brown. Transfer the cooked beignets to the baking sheet and keep frying until you have used all the batter, then serve on platters with small bowls of Mango-Ginger Chutney for dipping or use as a garnish with the beignets.

Crabmeat Prentiss

SERVES 8

Named for Susan and Bill Prentiss, this specialty may also be offered as a a dip served with croutons or crackers.

Small baguette of French bread
1/4 cup unsalted butter
1 cup finely chopped onion
1/2 cup finely chopped celery
1/2 cup finely chopped green bell pepper
1 small clove garlic, very finely chopped
1 pound cream cheese, at room temperature
1 cup sour cream
1 pound jumbo lump crabmeat, picked over and all bits of shell and cartilage removed
2 teaspoons Creole seasoning spice mix such as Tony Chachere's or Chef Paul's, (or your own from recipe on page 218)
2 green onions, white and green parts, thinly sliced
1/4 cup finely chopped fresh parsley
1/2 cup grated Parmesan cheese
1 cup grated Swiss cheese
Parsley sprigs, for garnish

Preheat the oven to 350°. To make the croutons, slice the baguette into 1/4-inch rounds. Arrange the slices on a baking sheet and toast just until pale golden. Turn and brush the other side lightly with olive oil, toast again until golden and set aside.

In a large saucepan, melt the butter over medium-low heat. Add and sauté the onion, celery and bell pepper until translucent, about 7 minutes. Add the garlic and cook for a minute or two, until tender but not browned. Add the cream cheese and sour cream and stir constantly until the cream cheese melts and the mixture comes to a simmer. Gently stir in the crabmeat, reduce the heat to very low and simmer for 3 minutes.

Add the Creole seasoning, green onions, parsley, Parmesan and Swiss cheese. Stir together to blend and bring just to a boil, then remove from the heat.

Divide the mixture among individual ramekins or shallow serving dishes and place on a plate with several croutons alongside each one, for scooping. Garnish with the parsley sprigs and serve hot.

Trout Mousse

SERVES 12 TO 16 AS AN HORS D'OEUVRE

The late chef Tom Cowman popularized this appetizer in the early 1980s. This still spectacular version has been simplified for the home kitchen and can be placed in a fish-shaped mold or a small loaf pan. The dill sauce relies on fresh dill to achieve its maximum potential—please don't use dried dill.

1 cup dry sherry
1 medium onion, coarsely chopped
1 bay leaf
3 stalks celery, coarsely chopped
1 teaspoon Kosher or sea salt
Scant 1/2 teaspoon ground white pepper
1 pound trout fillets (flounder or sole may be substituted)
1 cup mayonnaise
1 tablespoon fresh lemon juice
2 tablespoons Arnaud's Creole Mustard
1/2 teaspoon Tabasco Sauce
1 teaspoon chopped fresh tarragon leaves
1 teaspoon chopped fresh dill
2 teaspoon gelatin powder, stirred into 2 tablespoons hot tarragon vinegar, until smooth
1 tablespoon grated onion
1 teaspoon onion salt
24 to 32 thin slices of French bread, toasted and buttered, for serving
Dill Sauce, for serving (recipe at right)

In a saucepan, combine 1 cup of water, the sherry, onion, celery, bay leaf, salt and white pepper. Place over medium-high heat and simmer for 10 minutes.

Place the fish in a poaching pan and strain the stock over the top. Place the poaching pan over low heat and bring the liquid to a bare simmer. Cover and poach the fish for 10 minutes, or until it flakes easily.

Transfer the fish to a food processor and purée until smooth, adding just enough poaching liquid to make a moist purée. Transfer to a large mixing bowl and thoroughly stir in the mayonnaise, lemon juice, mustard, Tabasco, tarragon, dill, grated onion, onion salt and the gelatin mixture.

Line a 3-cup fish mold or loaf pan with plastic wrap, leaving the edges hanging out at least 3 inches all around. With a rubber spatula, fill the pan with the mousse mixture, smoothing it into the corners. Tap the mold on the counter to eliminate any air bubbles and cover the top with the overhanging plastic wrap. Refrigerate overnight, or until firm (at least six hours).

To unmold, dip the mold or pan into hot water for about 30 seconds, taking care not to allow any water into the pan. Unwrap the top, opening the plastic out to the sides, and place an appropriately sized and shaped platter upside down directly on top. Quickly and confidently invert the two together and give a downward shake to release the mousse onto the platter.

Serve with the toasted and buttered bread and the Dill Sauce.

Dill Sauce

YIELD: SCANT 1-3/4 CUPS

1-1/2 cups mayonnaise
2-1/2 tablespoons fresh lemon juice
3 tablespoons finely chopped fresh dill
1-1/2 tablespoons white wine vinegar
1-1/2 tablespoons Creole or other hot mustard, or to taste
1/2 teaspoon onion powder
6 drops Tabasco Sauce, or to taste

In a small bowl, whisk together all the ingredients. Cover and chill for at least 1 hour, and up to 4 hours, for the flavors to meld completely.

Crab-Artichoke Balls

YIELD: 6 DOZEN CANAPES

14 ounce can artichoke hearts, well drained
1 pound jumbo lump crabmeat, picked over for bits
    of shell
1 large egg, lightly beaten
1 tablespoon finely chopped fresh basil leaves
1 tablespoon chopped fresh thyme leaves, or 1
    teaspoon dried thyme
1/2 cup grated Parmesan cheese
Juice of 1/2 lemon
1/4 teaspoon ground white pepper
1/4 teaspoon freshly ground black pepper
1/4 teaspoon Cayenne pepper
1 teaspoon Kosher or sea salt
2 cups fresh bread crumbs

COATING

1 cup all-purpose flour
1/2 teaspoon granulated garlic
1/2 teaspoon Kosher or sea salt
1/8 teaspoon ground white pepper
1/8 teaspoon freshly ground black pepper
1/8 teaspoon Cayenne pepper
1 large egg, lightly beaten
1 cup fresh bread crumbs
Vegetable oil, for deep frying

In a food processor, purée the artichokes hearts until smooth, scraping down the sides of the bowl as necessary to make a very fine purée. In a large bowl, combine the artichoke purée, crab, egg, herbs, Parmesan, lemon juice, the three peppers, salt and breadcrumbs. Using clean hands, combine the mixture thoroughly. Cover and chill for at least one hour and up to six hours, to firm the mixture.

Again with clean hands, pinch up and form balls about 1 inch in diameter. If desired, place on a baking sheet, cover with plastic wrap and refrigerate for up to 8 hours before coating and frying. The balls may be held, refrigerated, until time to cook, up to a day ahead and shake off excess.

Half fill a deep, heavy pot or an electric deep fryer with oil and heat the oil to 375°. Place a large baking sheet lined with a double layer of paper towels in the oven and heat to its lowest setting.

Place three shallow bowls on the counter and in one, mix together the flour, granulated garlic, salt and the three peppers thoroughly. In the second bowl, beat the egg with 3 tablespoons of water. Place the breadcrumbs in the third bowl.

Dredge each ball first in the seasoned flour, shaking off any excess, and then dip in the egg mixture, letting any excess drain for a moment. Finally, dredge the balls in the breadcrumbs, pressing gently to help them adhere evenly.

In batches of about 10 balls, deep fry in a wire basket for about 90 seconds, until golden brown. Transfer to the baking sheet and keep frying until all the balls are golden brown. Serve at once.

Mushrooms Véronique

Yield: **60** APPETIZERS, OR "BITES"

There is rarely a mushroom left when these appetizers are presented. Not only are they very simple to prepare, they are an excellent crowd offering. Considering allergies and diets, Mushrooms Véronique is high in protein and uses no shellfish, fin fish, meat or nuts—the usual food allergy and diet adverse ingredients.

60 white button or crema mushrooms, about 1 inch in diameter, stems removed (save the stems for soup, if desired)
60 white seedless grapes, washed
15 ounces Boursin au Poivre soft cheese (three 5 ounce packages), at room temperature
1 cup clarified butter, warm (see page 206)
2 cups freshly grated Parmesan cheese

Preheat the oven to 425° and line one large or two smaller baking sheets with baking parchment.

Brush the mushrooms gently with a soft brush or paper towels to clean. In a large vegetable steamer set over simmering water (or a bamboo steamer set over a wok), steam the mushrooms rounded-side up for 3 minutes, to rid them of excess water. Cool.

Place the mushrooms rounded side down on a work surface and place one grape in the hollow of each cap. Scoop up about 1-1/2 teaspoons of the Boursin, and mound it over each mushroom cap, smoothing and completely enclosing the grape. Continue stuffing the remaining mushrooms. Place the Parmesan in a shallow bowl. With tongs, carefully dip each stuffed mushroom into the warm clarified butter, then dredge gently in the Parmesan. Gently shake off any excess and reserve the remaining Parmesan for another use.

Place the stuffed mushroom caps on the paper-lined baking sheet(s) and bake for 8 to 10 minutes, until golden brown. Serve at once.

Soups and Salads

A favorite location for small luncheons and dinner parties of 36 guests, the Bourbon Suites provide an opportunity to dine in an early Vieux Carré residence. Pocket doors divide the double parlors, which can slide into their hidden recesses in the walls, opening to each other and thereby creating one large room. The twin fireplaces face each other across the expanse. Kitchens were usually located in a dependency, a separate building tucked away in the back, to prevent any fires from spreading to the main house.

Creole cooks made a habit of keeping a stockpot simmering in order to have a basis for soup. Into the pot went any manner of bits and pieces of left-over meat, fish and vegetables. The stock would be strained, then used for the best recipes.

Salads made their appearance as an expedient way of using vegetables and rocketed to popularity with the creation of Caesar Salad in the 1920s. It found favor with the Duchess of Windsor, which went a long way toward spreading its popularity as chefs across Europe scrambled to offer her their version.

The late Julia Child tracked down the origins of Caesar Salad and remembered enjoying one as a young child with her parents at Caesar Cardini's Restaurant in Tijuana, Mexico. Tijuana's proximity to nearby Los Angeles put it within easy range of many movie stars, who also made a point of visiting for a Caesar Salad.

Interest created by these celebrity endorsements led to the acceptance of Caesar Salad as a restaurant menu item, presented a stage for further original salad and dressing productions and evolution as an entrée.

The property is noted on the De la Tour map (see page 220) which is the first survey that divides French Quarter blocks into numbered lots. The building was a series of night clubs until Casbarian joined it to his other structures and created the Bourbon Suites on the second floor with Café Remoulade on the first floor.

Seafood Courtbouillon

SERVES 4

Bouillabaisse—the famous fisherman's stew from the port cities of the Mediterranean, most notably Marseilles—was originally prepared from the unsold daily catch. It is endlessly variable, and many substitutions may be made while still maintaining the character of the original.

Long ago New Orleans cooks cheerfully embraced this notion, adding an abundance of local shellfish and crustaceans to what had been essentially a stew of fin fish. Along the way, the name changed, too. Now, New Orleans' version is known as Courtbouillon (say coo-bee-yon*). This is Louisiana's royal seafood broth, the bouillon of kings.*

Feel free to use any fresh seafood that is available, but maintain a balance of fin fish, shellfish, and crustaceans for a colorful variety of textures and flavor. Lobster is a luxurious top note, or can be used wherever fresh crawfish is unavailable. Scallops and 1/4-inch thick slices of grilled andouille sausage also make succulent additions.

1 tablespoon clarified butter (see page 206)
4 (2 ounce) trout fillets, cut into 2-inch pieces
12 shell-on shrimp, heads removed (about 1/2 pound at 21/25-count)
20 raw oysters, freshly shucked if possible
1 cup Crab or fish stock (see page 204)
8 Little Neck clams, scrubbed
8 mussels, scrubbed
1 cup fresh, peeled crawfish tails (about 20 tails), if available
1/4 pound jumbo or lump crabmeat, picked over
1 cup Creole Sauce (see page 161)
2 green onions, white and light green part only, finely chopped
4 tablespoons finely chopped flat-leaf parsley
1-1/2 teaspoons Kosher or sea salt
Freshly ground black pepper
4 (1/2-inch thick) slices of French baguette, toasted until golden
1/4 cup Lemon Butter sauce (see page 206)
Rouille (recipe follows), for serving

Place a large sauté pan over high heat and add the clarified butter. When it is hot, add the fish, shrimp and oysters and sear for one minute only. Drizzle in the crab stock and stir to deglaze the pan slightly, then add the clams and mussels and cover the pan. Reduce the heat to medium and cook until the clams and mussels open, 5 to 6 minutes. Discard any shellfish which have not opened after nine minutes. Add the crawfish, crabmeat and Creole Sauce and bring to a boil, then lower the heat to medium. Cover and simmer for two minutes, then stir in the green onions, parsley, salt and pepper and cook for three minutes more.

Ladle the soup, with plenty of assorted fish, into oversized soup or pasta bowls and garnish with the toasted baguette slices. Serve immediately, passing the Lemon Butter and Rouille at the table, or spoon a nice dollop of each sauce on top of each crouton.

ROUILLE
1 cup fresn bread crumbs
2 tablespoons chimayo chili, or 2 teaspoons chili powder
1 garlic clove
3/4 cup olive oil

In a food processor, combine ingredients and pulse to blend. Set aside.

Former Orleanians dream of fresh Louisiana oysters poached in a simple broth of milk, cream and butter and sparkling with delicate seasonings. The clarity of flavor is a bright and shining example of the region's best shellfish. Those of us who live here count oyster soup as one of our blessings.

Oyster Soup

SERVES 4 TO 6

3-1/2 cups water
2 dozen freshly shucked oysters, drained
1/2 cup chopped celery
1/2 cup chopped green onions
1/2 cup chopped onion
1 tablespoon plus 1/4 cup unsalted butter
1/2 teaspoon finely chopped garlic
1/8 teaspoon dried thyme
1/8 teaspoon ground red pepper
1 bay leaf
3/4 cup heavy cream
2 cups whole milk
1/2 cup all-purpose flour
1 teaspoon Kosher or sea salt
1/4 teaspoon ground white pepper

Bring water to a boil in a medium saucepan. Add oysters and cook for 3 minutes. Remove oysters with a slotted spoon and reserve 3 cups of liquid. Set both aside.

In a Dutch oven over medium heat, cook celery, green onions and onions in 1 tablespoon butter, stirring constantly until tender. Stir in 2-1/2 cups of the reserved liquid, garlic, thyme, red pepper and bay leaf; bring to a boil. Stir in the cream, reduce the heat and simmer for 5 minutes. Stir in the milk and return to a simmer.

Melt the remaining 1/4 cup butter in a small saucepan over low heat. Add the flour, stirring until smooth. Cook 1 minute, stirring constantly, then cook gently for about 3 minutes more or until smooth (the mixture will be very thick).

Gradually add the flour mixture to milk mixture, stirring with a wire whisk until blended. Add oysters, salt and white pepper. Cook until thoroughly heated. Remove from the heat, discard bay leaf and serve immediately.

Turtle Soup

A splash of sherry poured at the table brings out the richness of turtle soup. The addition of sherry is another local point of difference. Some cooks add the sherry during the cooking process, others when it is served and some prefer their turtle soup with no sherry at all.

Serves 6 to 8

1 gallon (4 quarts) water

3 pounds turtle meat or veal shoulder, or a combination of both, including any bones available

3 bay leaves

3 whole cloves

Zest of 1 lemon, finely chopped

1 tablespoon Kosher or sea salt

1/2 teaspoon whole black peppercorns

1 cup (8 ounces, 2 sticks) unsalted butter

2/3 cup all-purpose flour

2 stalks celery, chopped

2 medium onions, chopped

1 small green bell pepper, stemmed, seeded, de-ribbed and chopped

2 cloves garlic, finely chopped

1/2 teaspoon fresh thyme leaves or 1/4 teaspoon dried thyme

1/2 teaspoon chopped fresh marjoram or 1/4 teaspoon dried marjoram

1 cup dry sherry

2 tablespoons Worcestershire sauce

1 cup tomato purée

1 teaspoon salt-free Creole Seasoning

1/2 teaspoon Tabasco Sauce

2 hard-cooked eggs, chopped

Leaves only from 1 bunch of flat-leaf parsley, well washed and chopped

5 ounces fresh baby spinach (about 4 cups, loosely packed) well washed and chopped

In a large stock pot, cover the turtle meat with the water and add the bay leaves, cloves, lemon zest, salt and black peppercorns. Place over high heat and bring to a boil, then immediately reduce the heat so the water simmers gently. Cook slowly for two hours.

Strain the stock, reserving the liquid and the meat separately. If necessary, add additional water or meat stock to make three quarts. When cool enough to handle, chop and shred the meat into small pieces and set aside.

In a large saucepan, use the butter and flour to make a medium-dark Roux the color of a well-used penny, (see page 216). When the Roux reaches the correct color, add the celery, onions, bell pepper and garlic, and cook, stirring occasionally, until the vegetables are soft, about 7 minutes. Add the thyme, marjoram, sherry, Worcestershire sauce and tomato purée and bring the mixture to a boil.

Lower the heat and add the Creole Seasoning and Tabasco. Whisk in the reserved stock and add the turtle meat. Simmer the mixture, stirring occasionally, for 30 minutes. Taste for seasoning and adjust with salt, freshly ground black pepper and/or Tabasco Sauce as desired. Add the egg, parsley and spinach leaves and simmer for 10 minutes more. Serve in wide, shallow bowls.

Crawfish Bisque

Serves 6

In Louisiana, an abundance of crawfish make preparation of this traditional country fare a family weekend event: first, boil a big batch of mudbugs and enjoy hot from the pot; then, pick the meat from the leftover crawfish, make the stuffing and clean and stuff the heads. Finally, the rich, dark bisque is prepared.

Crawfish Boulettes can take the place of the stuffed crawfish bodies, simplifying the preparation without sacrificing richness or depth of flavor.

Note that in areas where fresh crawfish are unavailable, lobster may be substituted.

ROUX
3 tablespoons bacon fat
3 tablespoons olive oil
3 tablespoons unsalted butter
1 cup all-purpose flour

BISQUE BASE
4 tablespoons unsalted butter
1-1/2 large onions, finely chopped
6 green onions, white part only, thinly sliced (save the green parts)
1 stalk celery, finely chopped
2 cloves garlic, very finely chopped
1 cup fresh, peeled crawfish tails, pulsed to a fine paste in a food processor
Green tops from 1 or 2 stalks of celery, finely chopped
3 green onions, green parts only, finely chopped
2 tablespoons very finely chopped parsley
2 bay leaves
1/2 teaspoon ground white pepper
1/2 teaspoon ground black pepper
Scant 1/2 teaspoon Cayenne pepper
2 teaspoons Kosher or sea salt, or to taste
1 cup clam juice
3-1/2 cups chicken stock, (see page 204) or water
1/2 cup dry white wine
2 teaspoons Worcestershire sauce
2 tablespoons fresh lemon juice
Remaining whole peeled crawfish tails (or from a 1-pound package)
Crawfish Boulettes (recipe at right, freshly made), for garnish

In a large pot, make a Roux with the bacon fat, olive oil, and flour according to the instructions on page 216. Continue to cook and stir the Roux while you prepare the bisque base—you are aiming for a medium-dark Roux and this process should take about 30 minutes.

In a saucepan, melt the butter over medium heat and add the onions, white part of the green onions and the celery. Cook, stirring frequently until the vegetables are softened and just slightly browned, 15 to 20 minutes. Remove from the heat.

Continue cooking the Roux watching it carefully until medium-dark. Keep a close eye on the Roux and during the last 10 minutes of cooking time, and stir constantly, or the mixture may suddenly scorch and you will have to start over.

As soon as the Roux is ready, quickly stir in the browned vegetables and add the garlic, puréed crawfish tails, celery tops, green parts of the green onions, parsley, bay leaves, white and black pepper, Cayenne and salt. Cook, stirring, for 10 minutes. Do not let the mixture scorch.

Stir in the clam juice, chicken stock, wine, Worcestershire and lemon juice. Bring to a slow simmer, cover the pan and cook gently for 1 hour. Strain through a fine sieve into a clean pan, pressing down hard on the solids to extract all the flavor.

Taste the bisque for seasoning and adjust to your taste. If the liquid appears a bit thin, simmer and reduce to desired thickness. Stir in remaining whole crawfish tails and simmer for 2 minutes more to warm them through. Ladle the soup into large, shallow bowls and garnish each bowl with 2 to 3 crawfish boulettes, in place of traditional stuffed crawfish heads.

Crawfish Boulettes

These delicate balls may be used as a garnish for crawfish bisque, if desired. Otherwise they make an excellent hors d'oeuvre and may also be served as a first course or entrée.

1 pound domestic crawfish tails (if using frozen imported, see sidebar note)
2 large egg yolks
2 tablespoons olive oil
1 medium onion, very finely chopped
1/2 cup very finely chopped seeded and de-ribbed red bell pepper
1 stalk celery, very finely chopped
2 large cloves garlic, very finely chopped
5 green onions, green parts only, very finely chopped
2 tablespoons very finely chopped flat-leaf parsley
1 teaspoon Worcestershire sauce
1 teaspoon prepared horseradish
2 dashes Tabasco Sauce
1 teaspoon Kosher or sea salt
1/2 teaspoon freshly ground black pepper
1/4 teaspoon ground white pepper
1/4 teaspoon Cayenne pepper
1/2 cup fine, dry breadcrumbs
Vegetable oil, for deep-frying
1 cup all-purpose flour
1 teaspoon Kosher or sea salt
1 teaspoon granulated garlic
1/2 teaspoon freshly ground black pepper
1/4 teaspoon ground white pepper
1/4 teaspoon Cayenne pepper
1 large egg
1 cup fine, dry breadcrumbs

In a food processor, purée the crawfish tails and the egg yolks until smooth.

Place a large skillet over medium-low heat and add the olive oil. Sauté the onions, red pepper and celery for about 10 minutes, until very soft. Add the garlic and cook for 1 minute, then add the crawfish-egg mixture and stir well. Remove from the heat and mix in the green onions, parsley, Worcestershire sauce, horseradish, Tabasco, salt, black pepper, white pepper, Cayenne and the bread crumbs. The mixture should hold together if you squeeze a golf ball-sized piece in your hand; if it's too loose, add a little more breadcrumbs until it will hold together.

Using clean hands, portion out and form 1-inch balls, squeezing to firm. Place on a platter and if desired, refrigerate for up to 2 hours before frying. Cover if refrigerated for more than 30 minutes.

Half fill a deep, heavy pot or an electric deep fryer with vegetable oil and heat the oil to 350°. Preheat the oven to its lowest setting and place a baking sheet lined with a double layer of paper towels inside.

In a large shallow bowl, combine the flour, salt, granulated garlic, black pepper, white pepper and Cayenne. Mix together with a fork. In a second bowl, beat the egg with 2 tablespoons of water. In a third bowl, place the bread crumbs. Dredge the balls first in the seasoned flour, shaking off the excess, then dip in the egg wash, and then coat with bread crumbs.

Fry the balls in batches until golden brown, about 2 minutes. Do not overcrowd or the temperature of the oil will drop too much and the balls will be greasy. Transfer to the warm oven when done, and keep frying until all the boulettes are golden brown, then serve on doily-lined platters, if desired.

Shrimp Bisque

SERVES 6 TO 8

Other shrimp bisque recipes may be simpler and quicker, but for authentic, rich flavor, this one is worth the extra steps.

1-1/2 pounds fresh, head-on shrimp
2 large tomatoes, cored and coarsely chopped
1/2 cup (4 ounces, 1 stick) unsalted butter
1 large onion, finely chopped
2 leeks, white parts only, well washed and finely chopped
1 stalk celery, finely chopped
2 shallots, finely chopped
2 cloves garlic, very finely chopped
1/2 teaspoon fresh thyme leaves
4 tablespoons tomato purée
1/4 cup brandy
1 cup long grain rice
Kosher or sea salt and ground white pepper
1 long, fireplace match

Rinse the shrimp well, then peel them, and devein if necessary (if the vein is large and dark). Save all the heads and shells for the stock and refrigerate the shrimp bodies until needed.

Make the shrimp stock: Place the shrimp heads and shells in a large pot and cover with 2-1/2 quarts of water. Bring to a boil over high heat, then lower the heat and simmer gently until reduced to about 2 quarts. (You may skip this step by substituting 2 quarts chicken or other flavorful fish stock.)

In a medium saucepan, combine 1 quart of the stock with the chopped tomatoes and simmer gently, uncovered, for 30 minutes. While the stock is simmering, melt the butter in a large saucepan over low heat and sauté the onions, leeks and celery until softened and translucent, about 5 minutes. Add the shallots, garlic and thyme and sauté for 5 minutes more. Add the tomato purée and cook, stirring often, until slightly browned. Do not let the tomato paste scorch.

Add the brandy and stir to deglaze for just a moment, then ignite the brandy with a long match. When the flames die down, add the reserved shrimp, rice, tomato broth, and the remaining 1 quart of shrimp stock. Stir well and simmer the soup uncovered for about 30 minutes, until the rice is tender.

In batches, purée the soup in a food processor or blender, returning the puréed bisque to a large, clean pan. Simmer gently over very low heat for 20 minutes more, then strain through a fine sieve, and serve in cream soup bowls (with handles), or in large shallow bowls.

Oyster and Artichoke Soup

SERVES 6 TO 8

The late chef Warren LeRuth made a big mark in the culinary community by playing on the natural affinity between oysters and artichokes. The soup is prepared two ways in the city's restaurants: with cream and without. Warren's "Potage LeRuth" had no cream. This one has just a touch. Warren was a mentor to dozens of chefs and restaurateurs.

1 pint of shucked oysters, with their liquor
1 lemon, quartered
1 small onion, thinly sliced
2 sprigs fresh thyme
2 bay leaves
3 (15 ounce) cans of artichoke bottoms
1 teaspoon Kosher or sea salt
1/4 teaspoon freshly ground black pepper
1/4 cup (2 ounces, 1/2 stick) unsalted butter
2 tablespoons all-purpose flour
1-1/2 cups heavy cream
1/2 teaspoon Tabasco Sauce

Drain the oysters, reserving their liquor, rinse them and set aside. Strain the oyster liquor into a large saucepan and add enough water to make six cups. Rinse the artichoke bottoms well in a colander under cool, running water. Purée half the artichoke bottoms and finely dice the other half. Set the diced bottoms aside.

In another large saucepan, make a blond Roux from the butter and flour (see page 216).

Meanwhile, divide the oysters in half, keeping the big, good-looking ones for the garnish. Chop the remaining, smaller oysters. Stir in the cream, chopped oysters, puréed artichokes, diced artichoke bottoms and Tabasco. Bring the soup to a simmer and taste for seasoning. Add the whole oysters and simmer for only two minutes more. Ladle into bowls, distributing the whole oysters evenly.

Salad Sheila, with Chicken or Shrimp

This crisp salad is a perfect hot, sultry summer entrée, either at lunch or for a light supper. It is named for Sheila Bellaire. We offer two variations: grilled (or boiled) shrimp or chicken, or a combination of the two. Choose a firm head of iceberg lettuce for the "bowl" and a medium shrimp for grilling.

FOR CHICKEN:

SERVES 2

1 very crisp head iceberg lettuce
2 whole small skinless and boneless chicken breasts, trimmed of all fat
2 tablespoons Cajun seasoning mix
3/4 cup blue cheese dressing (store-bought or home-made, see page 90)
1 tablespoon finely chopped parsley, for serving
Lemon wedges, for serving

Cut the head of lettuce in half through the core. Carefully hollow the lettuce half, making two bowls with walls approximately 1/2-inch thick. Reserve the lettuce from the inside. If a bowl is too wobbly, carefully slice off a thin circle from the base, taking care not to cut through into the inside of the bowl.

To help the chicken breasts cook quickly and evenly, slice them in half horizontally, holding the top with the flat palm of your hand to help keep the two halves to an even thickness.

Rub both sides of each piece of chicken with a good pinch of the Cajun seasoning.

Pan-broil or grill the breasts over a medium-hot charcoal or gas fire for 3 to 4 minutes per side, until firm and done through to the center (if unsure, cut one open to test for doneness).

Cut the chicken into 1-inch chunks and place in a large bowl with the reserved shredded lettuce. Add the blue cheese dressing and toss together quickly. Pile into the iceberg bowls and sprinkle with parsley. Serve immediately, with lemon wedges on the side.

FOR SHRIMP:

SERVES 2

1 very crisp head of iceberg lettuce
1 pound 25/30 shrimp, peeled
1 tablespoon liquid crab boil (optional, if boiling shrimp)
4 tablespoons Kosher or sea salt
3/4 cup blue cheese dressing (store-bought or home-made, see page 90)
1 tablespoon finely chopped parsley, for serving
Lemon wedges, for serving

Follow directions to the left for creating lettuce bowls.

If grilling the shrimp: Sprinkle with Cajun seasoning and pan-grill or grill over hot charcoal for 2 to 3 minutes per side, until pink and opaque. Let cool to room temperature and refrigerate until chilled, about 1 hour.

If boiling the shrimp: Bring 2 quarts of water to the boil in a large pot with the crab boil and a pinch of salt. Place a large bowl of cold water and ice near the sink. Add the shrimp to the boiling water, cover the pot, and return to a boil. Boil for one minute, then drain the shrimp and plunge into the iced water to stop the cooking and quickly chill the shrimp.

Shred the reserved lettuce and place in a medium mixing bowl. Add the cooled drained shrimp and the blue cheese dressing. Toss together quickly and pile into the iceberg bowls.

Sprinkle the salads with parsley and serve immediately, with lemon wedges on the side.

Shrimp Maque Choux Salad

SERVES 6

Maque Choux are Indian words (say mock shoe) *meaning a spicy smothered corn dish. Early settlers, the Acadians from Canada, were introduced to corn by the resident Indian tribes. This recipe adds shrimp to the combination and creates a well-seasoned salad.*

1 lemon, halved
4 tablespoons Kosher or sea salt
1-1/2 teaspoon Cayenne pepper
4 cloves garlic, sliced
2 pounds peeled shrimp, deveined if necessary (if the vein is dark)
1/3 cup olive oil
1 large green pepper, stemmed, seeded, de-ribbed and cut into 1/4-inch dice
1 large red pepper, stemmed, seeded, de-ribbed and cut into 1/4-inch dice
2 cups frozen corn, thawed, or fresh kernels cut from 3 to 4 ears
1 red onion, cut into 1/4 inch dice
2 tablespoons finely chopped fresh cilantro (optional)
Kosher or sea salt
1 teaspoon ground white pepper
1 teaspoon Tabasco Sauce
Juice of 1 lime
Bibb lettuce and radicchio leaves, for serving

In a large saucepan, bring 1 quart of water to a boil. Squeeze in the juice of the two lemon halves and add the salt, Cayenne and garlic. Lower the heat and simmer for 5 minutes to blend the flavors. Add the shrimp, return to a boil and cook for 1 minute. Remove the pan from the heat and let stand, uncovered, for 5 minutes, to gently finish cooking. Drain and set the shrimp aside.

Place a large skillet over medium-low heat. Add the olive oil and, when it is hot, add and sauté the green and red peppers, corn and onion until only just wilted, about 5 minutes. Do not brown.

Remove the pan from the heat and let cool for 5 minutes, uncovered. Stir in the cilantro, a little salt, the pepper and the lime juice. Add the shrimp and toss gently to combine. If desired, cover with plastic wrap and refrigerate for one hour before serving.

Taste for seasoning and serve over whole leaves of Bibb lettuce and radicchio.

Mr. Dickey's Salad

Serves 8

Dickey Smith (aka Mr. Dickey) is the owner of the Guy Keefer Salon in the Royal Orleans Hotel. The beautiful people from across the city and around the country flock there for the fun and special attention that he provides as part of the atmosphere.

When appetites yearn for fresh, cool tastes, Mr. Dickey's Salad is crisp and tender, tart, sweet and light.

The chicken breast is marinated overnight in cilantro and lemon juice before grilling. Then, the sliced breast tops a salad of garden-fresh baby spinach, Stilton, golden raisins, spiced pecans, assorted vegetables and sun-dried tomatoes tossed in a pepper jelly-infused balsamic vinaigrette.

2 cups olive oil
1/2 cup lime juice (from about 3 fresh limes)
1 cup chopped fresh cilantro
8 boneless and skinless chicken breast halves
2 bags (or 2 bunches) fresh baby spinach leaves, thoroughly rinsed and spun dry
1 medium carrot, cut into julienne
1 small red onion, thinly sliced
1 cucumber, peeled, seeded, and cut into 1/4-inch dice
1/4 cup golden raisins
1/4 cup minced sun-dried tomatoes
1/2 cup Spiced Pecans (recipe follows)
1/4 cup crumbled Stilton cheese
Pepper Jelly Balsamic Vinaigrette, as needed (recipe follows)

In a baking dish, combine the olive oil, lime juice and cilantro. Add the chicken breasts and turn to coat both sides evenly. Cover with plastic wrap and refrigerate for about 24 hours, turning the breasts over several times.

Build a fire in a barbecue grill and allow the charcoal to burn until the briquettes are uniformly covered in gray ash.

While the coals are still too hot to grill, make the salad: Place the spinach leaves in a very large bowl. Add the carrot, onion, cucumber, raisins, sun-dried tomatoes, spiced pecans and Stilton. Set aside in the refrigerator while you cook the chicken.

Remove the chicken from the marinade and season both sides lightly with salt and pepper. Grill the chicken, turning once or twice, until only just firm and opaque through to the center; do not overcook. Transfer the cooked breasts to a cutting board and slice each one on the diagonal.

Toss the prepared salad gently, just to combine. Drizzle with about 1/2 cup dressing, just enough to lightly coat—but not drown—the greens. Mound onto individual plates.

Lift each sliced chicken breast with a wide spatula and place on top of each salad. Pass the remaining dressing at the table, in a small pitcher.

Spiced Pecans

These Pecans add crunch and a bit of sass to Mr. Dickey's Salad. The recipe makes enough to nibble on later with drinks, or while you're in the kitchen.

3 tablespoons unsalted butter, plus extra for the baking sheet
3 tablespoons granulated sugar
1 teaspoon Cayenne pepper
1/2 teaspoon ground ginger
2 tablespoons water
1-1/2 cups pecan halves

Preheat the oven to 350°. In a 10-inch sauté pan or skillet, melt the butter over medium-high heat. Stir in the sugar, Cayenne and ginger. Stir and cook for about 2 minutes, or until the sugar begins to dissolve. Stir in the water and cook for 1 minute more. Add the pecans and gently toss until they are coated with the glaze. Spread on a buttered baking sheet and toast in the oven for 5 minutes, or until the nuts are golden and the sugar has caramelized.

Keep any unused pecans in a tightly covered container for up to three months.

Pepper Jelly Balsamic Vinaigrette

YIELD: ABOUT 1-1/2 CUPS

1 large egg yolk
1/4 cup balsamic vinegar
1 cup plus 2 tablespoons olive oil
4 teaspoons pepper jelly
1/2 teaspoon Tabasco Sauce
4 teaspoons finely chopped shallots
Salt and freshly ground pepper

In a small bowl, whisk the egg yolk until pale. Whisking constantly, drizzle in the vinegar and oil, alternating, until smooth. Add the pepper jelly, Tabasco, shallots, and salt and pepper to taste. Use immediately, or cover and refrigerate for up to 24 hours. Bring to room temperature and whisk again before dressing the salad.

Blue Cheese Dressing

YIELD: ABOUT 4 CUPS

1 cup mayonnaise
1/3 cup sour cream
2 teaspoons red wine vinegar
2 teaspoons fresh lemon juice
1/4 teaspoon Tabasco Sauce
1-1/2 cups crumbled blue cheese
1/3 cup heavy cream
2 tablespoons very finely chopped flat-leaf parsley
1/4 teaspoon Kosher or sea salt
1/4 teaspoon ground white pepper

In a large mixing bowl, whisk the mayonnaise and sour cream together until light and fluffy. Whisk in the vinegar, lemon juice and Tabasco, then add the blue cheese and heavy cream and whisk until thickened; most of the large lumps of cheese should be dispersed. Add the salt and pepper and taste for seasoning. Cover and refrigerate for at least 2 hours to allow the flavors to blend, and up to 1 week. Use to dress sturdy salad greens, tomatoes, raw or lightly cooked vegetables, or as desired.

Arnaud's Creamy House Dressing

YIELD: 2-1/2 CUPS

1 cup mayonnaise
1/4 cup Creole mustard, preferably Arnaud's brand
1/2 cup olive oil
Dash each of Worcestershire sauce and Tabasco
1 tablespoon chopped garlic
2 teaspoons chopped anchovies
1 tablespoon finely chopped flat-leaf parsley
1 tablespoon green onions, chopped
1/3 cup red wine vinegar
1 tablespoon lemon juice
Dash each of salt and black pepper

With mixer at low speed, add Creole mustard to mayonnaise and slowly add olive oil.

Add Worcestershire and Tabasco, garlic, anchovies, parsley and green onions. Add red wine vinegar and lemon juice, salt and pepper and mix to blend.

Prepare about an hour ahead of serving time for best flavor. If refrigerated, bring to room temperature before serving.

Dill Vinaigrette Dressing

YIELD: ABOUT 1-1/2 CUPS

1/4 cup white wine vinegar
1/2 teaspoon Kosher or sea salt
Freshly ground black pepper
1-1/4 cups extra-virgin olive oil
1 shallot, finely chopped
1 tablespoon very finely chopped dill

In a bowl, whisk together the vinegar, salt and 1/4 cup of the oil until smooth and thick. Whisk in the remaining oil, the shallot and dill. Cover and refrigerate for at least 2 hours, for the flavors to blend, and up to 1 week, before using to dress delicate salad greens, raw or cooked vegetables, or as desired.

Champagne Vinaigrette

YIELD: ABOUT 2-1/2 CUPS

1 large egg yolk
1/2 teaspoon Kosher or sea salt
1/3 cup champagne vinegar
1-1/2 cups extra-virgin olive oil
1 large shallot, finely chopped
8 leaves fresh basil, chopped
Coarsely ground black pepper

In a mixing bowl, whisk together the egg yolk, salt and 1 tablespoon of the vinegar until smooth.

Whisking all the time, slowly add the oil in a thin stream. Continue to whisk until the vinaigrette thickens to the consistency of mustard. Whisk in the remaining vinegar, alternating with the oil until you have used all the specified amounts.

Stir in the shallot, basil and pepper to taste. Refrigerate for at least 2 hours, to allow the flavors to blend, and up to 2 days. Lightly dress salad greens, raw or slightly-cooked vegetables, or as desired.

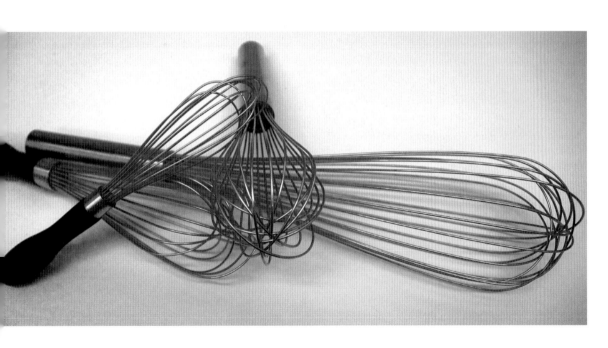

Brunch

The hospitality community in New Orleans has always been a small, close-knit family, enriched by fond and mutual respect. Count Arnaud used to tease his old friend Owen Brennan, who had also been a liquor salesman, by saying "What does an Irishman know about French food?" Owen called the Count's bluff and opened the now famous Brennan's of Royal Street in 1946.

Owen brought brunch to the forefront of American dining when he hatched the "Breakfast at Brennan's" concept. New Orleanian Frances Parkinson Keyes sparked Brennan's inspiration with her novel *Dinner at Antoine's*, published in 1948. Never one to let a good notion pass him by, Owen was quick to develop his own version of the idea.

It was a popular new beat to a beloved tune. With plenty of enthusiastic acceptance by celebration-minded Orleanians, the custom of a festive, weekend meal scheduled somewhere between breakfast and late lunch was enthusiastically embraced.

Germaine created her own Easter brunch and parade after attending New York City's event in 1954. The Friends of Germaine Wells carry on the tradition today, 50 years later. A parade of carriages and convertibles winds its way from Jackson Square to Arnaud's every Easter Sunday.

Poached Eggs Arnaud

SERVES 8 TO 10

At Arnaud's, this extravagant dish encompasses two selections from the poached egg menu in one serving. At home, any combination of these recipes would be delightful as well.

EGG-POACHING SAVVY

For a small group of guests, it is certainly practical to poach the eggs immediately before assembling the final dish. But to expedite preparation when entertaining a large group, poach the eggs up to a day ahead and reserve them, refrigerated, until just before serving. Such advance preparation will save time and reduce stress for hostesses.

To pre-poach 12 eggs: bring 2 quarts of water to a simmer in a large saucepan and add 4 tablespoons of white vinegar. Fill a large bowl with ice and water and place at the side of the stove.

Working two at a time so that you can easily keep track of the timing, quickly crack an egg into a small dish or saucer, then immediately slip it into the simmering water just above the water's surface and repeat with the second egg. Cook for 3 to 4 minutes, until the whites are just firm and the yolks are still quite soft to the touch. With a slotted spoon, gently retrieve the eggs and lower them into the iced water. Repeat with the remaining eggs, two at a time, leaving the eggs in the ice bath until all the eggs have been poached.

Gently retrieve the eggs and trim off any ragged edges with kitchen shears, returning them to the cold water. Cover the bowl securely and reserve for up to 24 hours in the refrigerator.

To warm the eggs at serving time, fill a large shallow dish or baking pan with 2 inches of boiling water and submerge the poached eggs, in batches if necessary, for 1 minute. Remove from the hot water bath with a slotted spoon, and rest the bottom of the spoon against absorbent towels briefly, to blot away any excess dripping water. Serve immediately, as directed in the recipe.

Eggs Benedict, Eggs Hussarde and Eggs Sardou are the most famous of the poached egg recipes.

Eggs Sardou

SERVES 6

12 freshly-cooked artichoke bottoms, still warm, or two 13.5 ounce cans, drained and rinsed
1 tablespoon unsalted butter (optional, only if using canned artichoke bottoms)
12 large eggs (or pre-poached eggs)
6 English muffins, split and toasted
1 cup Creamed Spinach (at right)
1-1/2 cups freshly-made Hollandaise Sauce (see page 208), kept warm in the top of a
    double boiler over hot—but not simmering—water
Dash of paprika

If using canned artichoke bottoms, melt the butter in a sauté pan over medium heat. Add the artichoke bottoms and cook gently, turning over once, for about 2 minutes, just to heat through without browning. Remove the pan from the heat, cover and set aside in a warm place (at the back of the stove, for instance).

Warm 6 dinner plates in a low oven and poach the eggs as described on page 95 (or warm 12 pre-poached eggs). Place 2 toasted muffin halves on each plate, cut side up, and place an artichoke bottom on each one. Spoon about 2 tablespoons of creamed spinach into each artichoke bottom, then place a poached egg on top. Ladle about 1/4 cup of Hollandaise Sauce over the top of each egg and sprinkle with a little paprika, for color. Serve immediately.

Creamed Spinach

SERVES 6 TO 8, YIELDS ABOUT 3 CUPS

2 (10 ounce) boxes frozen chopped spinach, completely thawed
4 tablespoons lightly salted butter
1 small onion, finely chopped
1 cup heavy cream
1 teaspoon Kosher or sea salt
1/2 teaspoon white pepper, preferably freshly ground
1/2 teaspoon ground nutmeg, preferably freshly ground
1 tablespoon cornstarch
4 ounce block of cream cheese

Using your hands, squeeze as much water as possible from the thawed spinach. In a large saucepan, melt the butter over medium heat. Sauté the onion, stirring occasionally, until tender, about 5 minutes. Stir in the cream and bring to a simmer. Add the spinach, salt, white pepper and nutmeg. Stirring occasionally, bring the mixture to a simmer, and cook for 3 minutes. In a small bowl, blend the cornstarch and 1 tablespoon of water until smooth. Add to the spinach mixture, then add the cream cheese and continue stirring until thickened, about 2 minutes. Taste for seasoning. Serve at once, or keep warm in the top of a covered double boiler over barely simmering water for up to 30 minutes. Or, cool to room temperature, cover and refrigerate. Reheat in a double boiler before serving.

Eggs Benedict

SERVES 6

When he acquired his very own venerable dining establishment, Casbarian wasted no time in launching Brunch and Jazz as an every-Sunday event at Arnaud's.

Since the seventies, brunch has become a favorite indulgence across the country. It's easy to understand why: a lazy, luxurious celebration of the week past and the one just ahead—a festive, family-oriented punctuation to the week.

12 large eggs (or 12 pre-poached eggs)
6 English muffins, split and toasted
12 slices Canadian bacon, warmed in a low oven
1-1/2 cups freshly-made Hollandaise Sauce (see page 208), kept warm in the top of a
**   double boiler over hot—but not simmering—water**
Dash of paprika
Sprigs of fresh curly parsley, for garnish

Warm 6 dinner plates in a low oven and poach the eggs as described on page 95 (or warm 12 pre-poached eggs). Place 2 toasted muffin halves on each plate, cut side up, and top each one with a slice of Canadian bacon. Place a poached egg on top of the bacon and ladle about 1/4 cup of Hollandaise Sauce over each. Sprinkle with a little paprika, for color and garnish each plate with a sprig or two of curly parsley. Serve immediately.

Eggs Hussarde

SERVES 6

4 tablespoons unsalted butter
12 large eggs (or pre-poached eggs)
3 cups freshly-made Hollandaise Sauce (see page 208), kept warm in the top of a
**   double boiler over hot—but not simmering—water**
3 cups Bordelaise Sauce (see page 207), kept warm in the top of a double boiler over
**   hot—but not simmering—water**
12 Holland rusks
12 slices Canadian bacon (ham may be substituted)
12 slices grilled tomato

Warm 6 dinner plates in a low oven and poach the eggs as described on page 95 (or warm 12 pre-poached eggs). Melt the butter in a large sauté pan and warm the Canadian bacon over low heat. Grill tomato slices under a hot broiler.

Place 2 Holland rusk on each plate. Top each one with a grilled tomato slice and poached egg. Ladle about 1/4 cup of Hollandaise Sauce and 1/4 cup of Bordelaise Sauce over each. Serve immediately.

Grillades and Grits

SERVES 4

Say gree-yahds. To keep cooked grits hot and creamy until serving time, set the covered pan inside a larger pan containing a couple of inches of hot water, over lowest heat.

The unfamiliar can get over their reaction to grits by thinking of them as New Orleans' version of polenta.

About 1-1/2 pounds veal or beef round, trimmed
2 teaspoons Kosher or sea salt
1 teaspoon freshly ground black pepper
1/8 teaspoon Cayenne pepper
3 cloves garlic, very finely chopped
2 tablespoons all-purpose flour
1-1/2 tablespoons lard
Half an onion, finely chopped
1 large, ripe Creole (beefsteak or Jersey) tomato, cored and coarsely chopped
1 cup water, or more, if necessary
2-1/2 to 3 cups hot, quick-cooking grits (not instant)

Cut the meat into 2-inches pieces and place between two sheets of plastic wrap, if desired, to avoid splattering as you pound. With a meat mallet, pound each piece out to about 4 inches square, keeping them as even as possible. In a large, shallow bowl, combine the meat with the salt, black pepper, Cayenne and garlic. With your hands (wear surgical gloves if desired) rub the seasonings evenly into both sides. Scatter the flour over the top and rub it in evenly.

Preheat the oven to 200°.

In a large heavy skillet or sauté pan, melt the lard over medium heat. When it is hot, brown the grillades on both sides, working in several batches to avoid overcrowding. Lower the heat and add the onion, tomato and water. Bring to a simmer, cover loosely, and cook over low heat for about 30 minutes, turning the meat over every 10 minutes. A rich brown gravy will form during the cooking; if it is too thick, add water a teaspoon or so at a time to thin slightly.

After 30 minutes, the meat should be tender. Transfer to a warmed platter and return to the turned-off oven to keep warm. Prepare the grits, if you have not already done so. If necessary, reheat the gravy in the skillet, then pour it over the meat and the grits.

TO SERVE WITH FRIED GRITS:

Generously butter an empty, very clean, standard-size food can with one end still in place. Spoon the prepared grits into the can and tap on the counter to settle. Smooth the top and compact the grits with a spoon, then refrigerate for at least 2 hours or overnight, to firm. To unmold, use a can opener to remove the remaining end of the can and push the cylinder of grits out onto the counter. Cut with a sharp knife into 1 to 1-1/2-inch thick patties. Sauté the patties in hot butter until light golden brown. Place one grits patty in the center of a warm plate, top with a grillade and some gravy, then stack with another grits patty, another grillade and more sauce. Garnish with finely chopped flat-leaf parsley.

Fried Cheese Grits

SERVES 4

Grillades and grits is a classic New Orleans brunch or supper dish. Arnaud's varies the standard presentation by serving grillades over fried cheese grits.

4 cups water
2 tablespoons unsalted butter
Kosher or sea salt
1 cup quick-cooking grits (not instant)
1/2 cup grated cheddar cheese
3/4 cup corn flour or all-purpose flour
Ground white pepper
1/2 cup clarified butter (see page 206) or unsalted butter, for frying

Lightly oil a 9 x 5-inch baking dish, or a loaf pan.

In a large saucepan, bring 4 cups of water, 1 teaspoon of salt and the butter to a boil over high heat. Slowly stir in the grits and immediately lower the heat so the water simmers very gently. Cook, stirring frequently, for 5 to 7 minutes or until thick and creamy. Stir in the grated cheese and continue to stir until the cheese melts smoothly into the grits. Remove from the heat and cool for 2 to 3 minutes.

Scoop the cooked grits into the prepared dish and smooth the top into an even layer. When the grits reaches room temperature, cover with plastic wrap and refrigerate overnight.

At serving time, turn the grits out of the dish or mold and cut into 1/2 inch patties. In a large shallow bowl or pie tin, combine the flour with a generous pinch of salt and white pepper. Dredge the patties lightly through the seasoned flour and shake off any excess.

Place a large skillet over medium-high heat and add the clarified butter. When it is very hot, fry the patties, in batches if necessary to avoid overcrowding, for about 1 minute on each side, until golden brown.

Variation: For a breakfast treat, make the grits ahead of time as described above, but substitute cream for half the specified amount of water. Continue with the recipe as above and serve alongside scrambled eggs, drizzled generously with your favorite syrup or sprinkled with sugar.

Red Bean Omelette

SERVES 6

Depending on your mood, make 2 medium-sized, or 1 large omelette. Carve as necessary according to the number of diners.

10 large eggs
1/4 cup water
Kosher or sea salt
White pepper, preferably freshly ground
2 tablespoons unsalted butter
2 cups cooked red beans (see page 155) or a 15 ounce can of red beans, preferably
    Blue Runner brand
2 cups grated cheddar cheese
8 green onions, white and light green parts only, finely chopped

In a bowl, combine the eggs, water, 1/2 teaspoon salt and a little pepper. Whisk energetically until the color is even.

Place a 10-inch non-stick skillet (or two smaller skillets) over medium-high heat and add the butter. When the butter has foamed, the foam begins to subside and the butter is just beginning to brown, tilt the pan to distribute the butter evenly and pour the egg mixture into the pan.

After 30 seconds, use the edge of a non-stick spatula to carefully push a little of the cooked edges toward the center, while still keeping the eggs in an even layer. The uncooked eggs will flow gently toward the edges and the omelette will cook more evenly. Continue to tilt the pan and gently move the cooked portions around the pan as necessary. When the center of the top is thickened and there is no more standing liquid, scatter half the red beans, the cheese, and about three-quarters of the chopped green onions evenly over the omelette. With the spatula, fold the top third of the omelette down over the center.

Fold the bottom third up towards the center to make an envelope shape. Let the omelette cook for about 30 seconds more, then turn out onto a platter and cut in sections. Transfer each portion to a plate and sprinkle with a little of the remaining red beans, grated cheese and chopped green onions. Serve immediately.

Brunch is a fine time to relish a red bean omelette. We also enjoy it as an evening meal served with a side of grilled sausage, a salad and hot bread.

Homemade Creole Cream Cheese

YIELD: ABOUT 1 QUART

Nothing evokes such passionate memories of long-ago delicacies like the mention of Creole cream cheese. Once a staple of the summer kitchen, it came about more by necessity than invention: Creole cream cheese was the end result of a hot, sultry climate, non-existent refrigeration and the Creole tradition against waste.

When the milk clabbered (a nice way of saying curdled or soured) the solids separated from the whey. The whey was drained off and the curds were hung in a muslin bag to drain. The concentrated cheese left in the bag was creamy and tangy then became the focus of a traditional Creole breakfast or brunch.

Louisiana state health regulations and a shrinking number of local dairies combined to spell a decline for this traditional foodstuff over the past few generations. But today, the practice of making Creole cream cheese is enjoying a renaissance. It's a delicious and easy home-made cheese that will evoke the flavors of times past in the Big Easy.

Note that rennet tablets can be obtained at a pharmacy.

2 rennet tablets (or 6 to 8 drops of liquid rennet)
1 gallon (4 quarts) skim milk
1 cup buttermilk

Dissolve the rennet tablets in 1/2 cup of warm (not hot) water, stirring.

In a large glass or stainless steel bowl (do not use aluminum!), combine the skim milk, buttermilk and rennet mixture. Stir to mix and cover with plastic wrap.

Let stand at room temperature for 24 to 36 hours, until the mixture separates into whey and curds. The large white curds will sink to the bottom of the container, while the watery, mostly clear whey will rise to the top.

Line a colander with 2 layers of slightly dampened cheesecloth, letting 2 inches hang over the edges of the colander. Place the colander over a large bowl and slowly pour in the curds and whey. The whey will drain off through the colander, leaving the curds in the colander to continue draining and solidifying. Cover the colander with plastic wrap and refrigerate for 48 hours. Use as directed in the recipe or keep in the refrigerator until needed, up to 1 week.

Victor Hugo Schiro (right) served as Mayor of New Orleans from 1961 to 1969 and made honoring Germaine a priority at the beginning of each Easter parade. She always began the event at her father's Esplanade Avenue mansion where Bloody Marys and cocktails got the ladies off to a rolling start. Germaine's late daughter, Arnaud (left), is seated beside her mother in the carriage.

Carriages continue to traverse the French Quarter. It is an excellent way to view the street scene and architecture.

Calas (Rice Cakes)

YIELD: ABOUT 1 DOZEN

Around the turn of the century, fresh, hot and aromatic Calas were sold from horse-drawn carts in the French Quarter. Sadly this tradition has all but disappeared—but with a little advance planning, Calas are easily made in the home kitchen. Attempts to streamline the process by using double-acting baking powder have been less than satisfactory and are certainly not authentic. To serve Calas for a special Sunday Brunch for a few lucky friends and family, begin the preparations on Saturday by cooking extra rice at dinner. Remember, the Creole cook wasted nothing—leftover rice was turned into delectable breakfast treats!

Note: neither the risen batter nor the Calas keep well, so cook them as soon as the batter rises and enjoy them as soon as they come from the oven.

1/4 cup hand-hot water (110°)
1 package instant dry yeast
1 teaspoon granulated sugar
2-1/2 cups cooked long-grain white rice
3 large eggs, lightly beaten
1/2 cup light brown sugar
1/4 teaspoon nutmeg, preferably freshly ground
1 teaspoon ground cinnamon
1/2 teaspoon Kosher or sea salt
1-1/2 cups all-purpose flour
Vegetable oil, for deep frying
Powdered sugar, for serving

In a large glass or ceramic bowl, combine the water, yeast, and sugar and stir with a fork. Let stand for 5 minutes, after which the yeast should begin to bubble (if it does not bubble, your yeast is dead and should be replaced). Add the cooked rice and beat with a wooden spoon for about 2 minutes until evenly blended. Cover the bowl with a kitchen towel and let stand in a warm place overnight, to rise.

In the morning, thoroughly mix the eggs, brown sugar, nutmeg, cinnamon, salt and flour into the risen rice mixture. If you have difficulty adding the dry ingredients because the mixture is too stiff, add just a little water, a few drops at a time, until you have an evenly blended, very thick batter that will hold its shape on the spoon. Cover with a kitchen towel and again, set aside in a warm place to rise for 30 minutes.

Place a platter lined with a doubled layer of paper towels in the oven and set it to the lowest heat.

Place a large, deep, and heavy saucepan no more than half full of vegetable oil over high heat and heat the oil to 375°.

Using two spoons, drop pieces of batter about the size of a large walnut into the oil. Fry 3 or 4 at a time, to avoid overcrowding, until dark brown, turning with tongs or a skimmer as needed to brown evenly.

Keep the finished Calas warm in the oven while you fry the remaining Calas. As soon as all the Calas are fried, sprinkle with powdered sugar and serve at once.

Pain Perdu (French Toast, aka Lost Bread)

SERVES 6

Lost Bread refers to the stale, day- or two day-old loaf: lost, until found again in a new guise. This popular dish was created by the Creoles as another way of making use of leftovers. While French bread is preferable, Italian or any other dense bread will work well. Sliced white bread may substitute in a pinch.

6 large eggs
3 tablespoons granulated sugar
1 tablespoon vanilla extract
1 cup whole milk
1/2 teaspoon ground cinnamon
1/4 teaspoon ground nutmeg
12 slices of French, Italian or other white bread, sliced 3/4-inch to 1-inch thick
1/2 cup (4 ounces, 1 stick) unsalted butter, melted, or vegetable oil
Powdered sugar, chopped roasted pecans, honey, pancake or cane syrup, for toppings
Applesauce, for garnish, if desired
Sliced or stewed fresh fruit such as strawberries, apples, pears, or bananas, if desired

In a large, wide and shallow bowl that is larger than the slices of bread, beat the eggs, sugar, vanilla, milk, cinnamon, nutmeg and milk, until smooth and evenly colored.

One or two at a time, soak the bread slices in the custard mixture for a little less than a minute on each side, so the bread absorbs some the liquid. Caution: the bread will get soggy and fall apart if left in the liquid too long.

Preheat the oven to the lowest heat and place a paper towel-lined platter and six brunch plates inside to warm.

Heat a large skillet or a griddle over high heat until a drop of water pops and skitters across the surface. Brush generously with the butter and add one batch of bread (how many slices per batch will depend on the size of the pan; do not crowd the slices). Fry for a minute or two on each side until golden brown and crispy. Transfer the finished pain perdu to the platter in the oven to keep warm while you fry the remaining slices. Add more butter as necessary and note that as more slices are cooked, you will have to lower the temperature to keep them from burning.

Sprinkle with powdered sugar or chopped roasted pecans, or drizzle with honey, syrup, or applesauce, if desired. Scatter with fresh fruit, if desired, and serve.

Arnaud's loaves of French cap bread make nice, large slices. If using the smaller baguette, slice on a diagonal at about 45-degrees instead of straight up and down, for a larger surface area.

Ladies in extravagant bonnets and finery appropriate to the day parade from Noon Mass at Saint Louis Cathedral to Arnaud's. Here, they sashay through the dining rooms following the Friends of Germaine Wells parade, tossing stuffed easter bunnies and candy-filled eggs to the restaurant's guests. A hat contest and brunch with their families and friends is another highlight of the day.

Seafood

The Count was fond of writing about food; its customs and preparation and the proper service, such as this revelation: "Cooking in New Orleans has a cachet all its own. C'est la cuisine Creole…although the delicacy and artistry of the French School predominates through it, it has also the piquancy and tang of the Spanish, with the simplicity and wholesomeness so much favored by the early colonists in America."

A bounty of seafood from the region's Gulf, lakes and rivers then and now kept New Orleans well supplied with shrimp, crabs, crawfish, a variety of fin fish and oysters. The large Catholic community supports the custom of serving fish on Friday. The meatless Lenten season between Mardi Gras and Easter Sunday also helps bring the readily available seafood to the table often.

Various species are impacted by commercial and sport fishing from time to time, but an abundance of other seafood is available to take their place. In keeping with the Creole habit of making substitutions from French and Spanish recipes, many seafood items can be replaced with another. For example, shrimp, crab, scallops or lobster can be used instead of crawfish in many dishes.

The Lafitte, Dauphine and Toulouse rooms are typical of Creole residences, demonstrating flexibility, as do Creole recipes. These rooms open and close to one another, standing as a trio, as a pair, or as one single dining room. Up to 56 guests may be accommodated by reserving all three rooms.

Speckled Trout Meunière

SERVES 6

1-1/2 cups Meunière Sauce, for serving (recipe follows)
Vegetable oil, for deep frying
6 skinless trout fillets, 6 to 7 ounces each, preferably speckled trout
1 cup all-purpose flour
Kosher or sea salt and freshly ground black pepper
1/2 cup whole milk
1/4 cup buttermilk
2 lemons, ends trimmed and cut into wedges, for serving
Sprigs of fresh flat-leaf or curly parsley, for garnish

Prepare or reheat the Meunière Sauce, if you have not already done so.

In an electric deep fryer or a large and deep, heavy saucepan or stockpot no more than half filled with oil, heat the frying oil to 350°.

Place the flour in a large, shallow bowl near the stove and season it generously with salt and pepper. In another large, shallow bowl combine the milk and buttermilk.

Place a baking sheet lined with a double layer of paper towels in a low oven, and warm six dinner plates and a serving platter.

Dredge two of the trout fillets in the seasoned flour, then dip in the buttermilk mixture, coating both sides evenly. Dredge again in the seasoned flour and gently shake off the excess.

Gently lower the two fillets into the oil. Cook for 4 to 5 minutes, until golden brown, nudging occasionally. Retrieve the fillets gently with a skimmer and transfer to the baking sheet. Dredge and fry the next two batches of fillets in the same way.

Transfer all the fillets to the hot platter and garnish with lemon wedges and parsley sprigs. Serve with the Meunière Sauce passed in a sauce-boat, on the side.

Meunière Sauce

YIELD: 2 CUPS

(The sauce will keep in the refrigerator for up to 1 week.)

3 tablespoons Medium-Dark Roux (see page 216)
2 tablespoons (1 ounce) unsalted butter
1/2 stalk celery, finely chopped
Half a white onion, finely chopped
1/4 cup finely chopped seeded and de-ribbed green bell pepper
1/4 cup finely chopped flat-leaf parsley
1/4 teaspoon freshly ground black pepper
1 bouquet garni (see page 217)
1 clove
1-1/2 cups Veal Stock (see page 205)
Juice of 1/2 lemon
Kosher or sea salt and freshly ground black pepper

Prepare the Medium-Dark Roux, if you have not already done so.

In a saucepan, melt the butter over high heat. Add the celery, onion, green pepper, parsley, black pepper, bouquet garni and the clove. Sauté until nicely browned, about 4 minutes, stirring occasionally. Add the veal stock and lemon juice and bring to a boil. Boil for 2 minutes, then lower the heat and simmer the mixture gently for 10 minutes.

Add a tablespoon of Roux and simmer for 2 to 3 minutes, until thickened. Keep adding Roux one tablespoon at a time until the sauce coats a spoon. Season to taste with salt and a little more black pepper, and strain into a clean saucepan (or directly into the sauceboat, if serving right away), pressing down on the solids and scraping the bottom of the sieve to retrieve as much sauce as possible.

Trout Amandine

This buttery combination of trout and sliced almonds is a New Orleans favorite that's directly descended from the French.

1 cup (8 ounces, 2 sticks) unsalted butter
1 cup blanched, sliced almonds
Juice of 1 lemon
1 tablespoon finely chopped flat-leaf parsley
Vegetable oil, for deep frying
6 skinless speckled trout fillets, about 8 ounces each
1-1/2 cups all-purpose flour
Kosher or sea salt and freshly ground black pepper
Finely chopped flat-leaf parsley, for garnish
Thin slices of lemon, for garnish

Heat the oven to its lowest setting a place a baking sheet lined with a doubled layer of paper towels inside. Place six dinner plates in the oven to warm.

In a small skillet, melt about 1/2 cup of the butter over low heat. Add the almonds and stir and turn gently until they are uniformly golden, 5 to 7 minutes. Remove the almonds from the pan with a slotted spoon, place in a bowl and set aside.

Add the remaining butter to the same skillet. When it is melted, stir in the lemon juice and parsley. Add salt and pepper to taste and taste for seasoning. Set aside while you fry the fish.

Place the flour in a large, shallow bowl near the stove and season generously with salt and pepper. In an electric deep fryer or a deep, heavy saucepan or stock pot no more than half filled with oil, heat the oil to 350°. Dredge two of the fillets in the seasoned flour, coating both sides. Shake off any excess flour and gently lower the fillets into the hot oil. When the first two fillets are golden brown, remove with a skimmer basket and transfer to the towel-lined baking sheet to drain and keep warm while you fry the remaining fillets in the same way. (Do not dredge the fillets until just before frying, or the coating will be gummy.)

Return the lemon-butter sauce to high heat and stir for a minute or two, until piping hot.

Place each fillet on a hot plate and scatter generously with the almonds. Drizzle with some of the lemon-butter sauce and serve at once.

One of the locals' favorites is to serve Trout Meunière and Trout Amandine together, on the same plate. These are two of New Orleans' prime fish dishes, and to sample them both together is a *tour-de-force*.

Pompano en Papillote

SERVES 4

Here is a fresh answer to that popular classic, yet old-fashioned heavy dish, pompano en papillote. In this recipe, the thick, chock-full-of-seafood sauce is replaced with a light collection of savory herbs. The papillote, or parchment enclosure, keeps the fish moist by essentially cooking it in its own steam. It is a light-hearted idea and the dish looks beautiful, too. Small salmon, flounder and freshwater trout also work well.

The parchment paper needed for this dish is more easily available than it once was, but can always be found at kitchen supply stores. Uncoated butcher paper may be used, but not aluminum foil, which will yield a metallic taste.

2 tablespoons unsalted butter, softened
1/2 cup green onions, green parts only, thinly sliced
1/2 stalk celery, cut into fine matchsticks
4 teaspoons finely chopped fresh dill
1 teaspoon finely chopped fresh tarragon
4 small, skinless filets of pompano, about 6 ounces each
Kosher or sea salt and freshly ground black pepper
2 tablespoons dry white wine
1 tablespoon fresh lemon juice

Preheat the oven to 375°.

Cut four large squares of parchment paper, as wide as the roll. Fold them in half and cut each one into half a heart shape. Open out the papers into full hearts and rub both inside surfaces with the softened butter.

Scatter about one eighth of the green onions, celery, dill, and tarragon on the right side of each parchment heart, to the right of the fold. Top each with a pompano filet and season with salt and pepper, then top equally with the remaining vegetables. Drizzle the white wine and lemon juice evenly over the ingredients.

Fold the left side of the parchment over the right, covering the ingredients. Starting at the top of each parchment heart, make small folds, crimping along to seal the pouch all the way down to the point of the heart.

Place the pouches on a baking sheet and bake for about 12 minutes. When the parchment has begun to brown, it's done. Place the pouches onto individual serving plates and have guests tear them open at the table. (Guests dine right out of the bag, which releases a delightful aroma when torn open.)

Pompano Duarte

SERVES 6

1/4 cup clarified butter (see page 206)
6 small, skinless pompano fillets, about 6 ounces each
3/4 cup Garlic Butter (recipe follows)
1 pound tiny shrimp, 31/30 count, peeled and deveined
1 teaspoon finely chopped fresh oregano
1 teaspoon finely chopped fresh thyme
1 teaspoon finely chopped fresh basil
Pinch of red pepper flakes
1 teaspoon coarsely cracked black pepper
1/2 cup canned peeled and diced tomatoes, drained
1 cup Beurre Blanc Sauce, warm (recipe follows)

GARLIC BUTTER

YIELD: 1-1/2 CUPS

1-1/2 cups (12 ounces, 3 sticks) unsalted butter, at
    room temperature
6 cloves garlic, very finely chopped
1/4 cup Herbsaint liqueur or Pernod
1 cup finely chopped fresh flat-leaf parsley
Kosher or sea salt and freshly ground black pepper

BEURRE BLANC SAUCE

YIELD: About 1 CUP

1/3 cup dry white wine
1/3 cup heavy cream
1 large shallot, very finely chopped
3/4 cup (6 ounces, 1 1/2 sticks) unsalted butter, cut into
    1/2-inch cubes and softened
1/2 teaspoon Kosher or sea salt
1/8 teaspoon white pepper, preferably freshly ground
2 tablespoons snipped fresh chives

Preheat the oven to low heat and place six dinner plates inside to warm. Assemble the Garlic Butter, herbs and spices, tomatoes and Beurre Blanc Sauce near the stove.

Place a very large skillet (or cook in batches) over high heat and add the clarified butter. Season the fillets with salt and pepper, and sauté, without crowding, for 2 to 3 minutes on each side, until golden (total cooking time will depend on the thickness of the fillets).

Transfer the pompano to a platter and keep warm in the oven, loosely covered with aluminum foil, while you make the sauce. Add the Garlic Butter to the same pan used for cooking the fish and place over medium heat. Add the shrimp and cook until they turn pink, about 2 minutes. Spoon off the excess butter from the pan and add the chopped herbs, red pepper flakes, black pepper and tomatoes. Cook for 2 minutes, stirring occasionally, and stir in the Beurre Blanc Sauce. Spoon the sauce and shrimp over the pompano and serve immediately, providing the hot plates at the table.

GARLIC BUTTER

In a food processor or an electric stand mixer, mix the butter until smooth. Add the chopped garlic and process until smooth, then add the Herbsaint, chopped parsley, and salt and pepper to taste. Mix until completely smooth and all the liqueur has been absorbed; this may take 3 to 5 minutes in a stand mixer, but will take less time in a food processor. Taste for seasoning and adjust if necessary.

BEURRE BLANC SAUCE

In a small saucepan, combine the wine, cream and shallot and place over medium-high heat. Bring to a boil, then reduce the heat to low. Simmer gently until reduced to about 2 tablespoons, watching carefully, about 10 minutes. Set aside for up to one hour before finishing the sauce, if desired, or finish immediately.

Place the pan over low heat to warm through, if necessary. As soon as it is steaming, add all the butter at once and swirl the pan or whisk the sauce continuously until the butter has been thoroughly absorbed and the sauce is smooth. Remove from the heat immediately, and stir in the pepper and chives. Use within 10 minutes or keep warm, covered, in the top of a double boiler over hot but not simmering water for up to one hour, stirring occasionally.

Grilled Red Snapper Mitchell

SERVES 4

Mitchell Hoffman has been Arnaud's attorney since Casbarian acquired the restaurant. His name graced Mussels Hoffman, which was dedicated to the slight gentleman. However, the dish was dropped from the menu. Snapper Mitchell was named to honor him and is more accurate.

This dish may be prepared on an outdoor grill or under a broiler. Note that the fire is ready when the coals are uniformly coated with gray ash.

4 (6 to 7 ounce) red snapper fillets
2-1/2 to 3 tablespoons extra-virgin olive oil
Kosher or sea salt and coarsely ground black pepper
5 ripe tomatoes, peeled, seeded and cut into 1/4-inch dice
1 clove garlic, very finely chopped
1/3 cup Kalamata olives, pitted and finely chopped
1 tablespoon finely chopped fresh basil
1 lemon, thinly sliced, for serving
2 tablespoons finely chopped flat-leaf parsley, for serving

Brush both sides of each fillet generously with olive oil, using about 1 tablespoon of the oil and season to taste with salt and pepper.

Preheat an outdoor grill to medium-high heat or an indoor broiler to high heat. (If using the broiler, and you have a separate oven, preheat the oven to 475°. If your oven and broiler are combined, you can switch to 475° immediately after the initial searing.) Assemble all the remaining ingredients near the stove.

Carefully place the fillets on the hot grill and cook for about 15 seconds, then give a quarter-turn and cook for 15 seconds more, to mark in a criss-cross pattern. Transfer the fillets to the coolest part of the grill surface and continue cooking until the fish is done through, firm, and opaque at the center, 3 to 4 minutes per side depending on the thickness of the fillets. (If using the broiler, transfer the fish to the preheated oven for 5 to 7 minutes, or switch the broiler function to oven and cook until firm and opaque.)

Transfer the cooked fillets to a platter and cover with aluminum foil. Set aside briefly in a warm place while you quickly assemble the sauce.

Place a small skillet over high heat and add the remaining olive oil. When the oil is hot, add the garlic and cook for no more than 10 seconds. Quickly stir in the tomatoes and cook for 1 minute, then add 1/2 teaspoon salt and black pepper to taste. Stir together to blend, then add the olives and basil, remove from the heat and stir together until evenly blended. Spoon the fresh tomato mixture over the fillets and garnish the platter with lemon wheels and chopped parsley. Serve at once.

Gulf Snapper Pontchartrain

SERVES 4

This simple, yet rich and elegant dish highlights freshly-caught snapper and succulent crabmeat. It's a dish that can be prepared successfully on an outdoor grill or in a hot skillet on the stove. Judge the doneness of the fish by poking it with your finger: If the fish is quite firm to the touch, it's probably done. Any doubts can easily be resolved by making a small cut to the center of the fillet; if the meat is opaque, the fish is safely cooked through.

4 (6 to 7 ounce) red snapper fillets
1 cup (8 ounces, 2 sticks) unsalted butter, melted
Kosher or sea salt and white pepper, preferably freshly ground
Juice of one lemon
2 teaspoons finely chopped flat-leaf parsley
1 cup lump crabmeat, picked over for bits of shell
Thin slices of lemon and parsley sprigs, for serving

Warm a platter in a low oven and preheat a grill, if desired, or place a large, heavy skillet over high medium-high heat.

Brush both sides of each snapper fillet with the melted butter, using about 1/4 cup. Season both sides to taste with salt and white pepper.

Place a small saucepan over high heat and add the remaining butter. Stir in the lemon juice, salt and white pepper to taste, and add the chopped parsley. Remove from the heat and set aside.

Grill or sauté the fish for 2 to 4 minutes per side, depending on their thickness, until done through, firm and opaque at the center. Transfer to the warm platter and cover with aluminum foil while you quickly finish the sauce.

Return the lemon-butter mixture to the heat and stir in the crabmeat. Toss gently for 1-1/2 to 2 minutes, just to warm the crabmeat through. Spoon the crabmeat butter sauce over the fillets, garnish the platter with lemon slices and parsley and serve at once.

Pompano David

SERVES 1, MULTIPLY AS NECESSARY BY THE NUMBER OF DINERS

Cooked outside on the grill or inside under the broiler, the fresh flavors of herbs and the mild pompano marry together perfectly, yielding a succulent, moist and delicate piece of fish. Other firm-fleshed fish, or raw, peeled jumbo-sized shrimp would also do nicely.

1 pompano fillet (about 8 ounces), with the skin on
1 teaspoon chopped fresh oregano
1 teaspoon chopped fresh thyme
1 teaspoon finely chopped garlic
1 teaspoon finely chopped fresh basil
1 tablespoon fresh lemon juice
Pinch of crushed red pepper
1 teaspoon coarsely cracked black pepper
2 tablespoons extra-virgin olive oil

Warm a dinner plate in a low oven.

Preheat an outdoor grill to medium-high heat, or an indoor broiler to high heat. Bring the pompano to room temperature for 5 minutes before cooking.

In a metal bowl, combine all the remaining ingredients and mix well. Brush both sides of the fish liberally with the seasoning mixture and place skin side-down the grill (or skin side-up under the hot broiler). Cover with a tin pan, a tent of aluminum foil or a pot lid large enough to cover the fish and cook for approximately 7 minutes, until firm.

Center the pompano fillet on a hot dinner plate and serve immediately.

Trout Marguery

SERVES 4

Even in a double boiler, this sauce may break down if you try to hold it for too long. Plan ahead and serve dinner as soon as the fish comes out of the oven.

4 skinless trout fillets
1 tablespoon extra-virgin olive oil
Kosher or sea salt and freshly ground black pepper
1 tablespoon unsalted butter, for cooking the mushrooms
1/2 cup mushrooms, brushed clean and sliced
1/4 pound medium shrimp, peeled and deveined if necessary
   (if the vein is large and dark), coarsely chopped
1/4 cup dry white wine
2 large egg yolks, lightly beaten
1 cup (8 ounces, 2 sticks) unsalted butter, melted and warm
2 tablespoons fresh lemon juice
1/2 cup lump crabmeat, picked over for bits of shell
Pinch of paprika

Preheat the oven to 375°.

Place the fillets in a glass or ceramic baking dish large enough to hold them without crowding and brush both sides evenly with the olive oil. Season both sides lightly with salt and pepper.

Bake the fish for 30 minutes, while you prepare the sauce: Place a small skillet over medium heat and add the butter. When it is melted and hot, add and sauté the mushrooms for 5 minutes, until softened. Add the shrimp and cook for 2 minutes, until just beginning to turn pink, then stir in the wine and simmer for 2 minutes, until most of the wine has evaporated. Remove the pan from the heat and set aside.

Place a double boiler over medium heat and bring the water to a bare simmer (the water should not touch the base of the upper pan).

Place the beaten egg yolks in the top of the double boiler and immediately begin whisking. Whisk just until the yolks thicken a tiny bit, so that you can see the base of the pan with each swipe of the whisk. As soon as this happens (continuing to whisk constantly) begin to add the melted butter a few drops at a time. When about 1/3 cup of the butter has been successfully incorporated into the egg yolks, begin adding butter just a little faster, in a very thin stream. When all the butter has been added and the sauce is nicely thickened, stir in the lemon juice, crabmeat, shrimp and mushroom mixture and the paprika.

Cover and cook very gently for about 5 minutes, stirring frequently, to heat all the ingredients through. Transfer the cooked fillets to a warm platter, nap each one with a generous spoonful of the sauce and serve at once.

Trout en Papillote

SERVES 2

6 ounces fresh spinach leaves (about 4 cups), washed (do not dry)
4 baby carrots, trimmed and peeled
10 asparagus tips
1 Idaho potato, peeled and sliced 1/4-inch thick
2 skinless trout fillets, 6 to 7 ounces each
Juice of 1 lemon
2/3 cup extra-virgin olive oil
2 or 3 cloves garlic, very finely chopped
4 leaves fresh basil, very finely chopped
Kosher or sea salt and freshly ground black pepper
1 tomato, halved, seeded and thinly sliced
1 roll parchment paper

Preheat the oven to 375°.

Bring a large saucepan of lightly salted water to a boil for blanching the vegetables.

In a skillet, wilt the spinach over medium heat, turning with tongs, for about 2 minutes. Blanch the vegetables one at a time, until crisp-tender, as follows: cook the carrots for about 10 minutes, the asparagus for about 5 minutes and the potatoes for about 5 minutes. As each one is cooked, retrieve with a skimmer, drain and refresh under cool running water to stop the cooking. Pat dry with paper towels.

In a glass or ceramic bowl, combine the lemon juice, olive oil, garlic, basil and a pinch each of salt and pepper.

Cut two large squares of parchment paper, as wide as the roll. Fold them in half and cut each one into half a heart shape. Open out the papers into full hearts and rub both inside surfaces with the seasoned oil. Place half the wilted spinach about 1 inch from the fold on the right side of each sheet. Place a trout fillet on top of the spinach, and layer half the blanched, drained vegetables over each fillet. Brush the vegetables with seasoned oil. Top with a few tomato slices and brush with any remaining oil.

Fold the left side of the parchment paper back over the fish and vegetables. Make small folds along the open edges of the paper in 3-inch lengths, to seal securely into a package.

Place the packages on a baking pan and bake for 20 minutes. Pull open the packages and slide the fillets and vegetables onto warm dinner plates.

Trout Véronique

SERVES 6

6 skinless trout fillets, about 6 ounces each
Kosher or sea salt and freshly ground black pepper
2 tablespoons unsalted butter
Véronique Sauce (recipe below), warm, for serving

Warm six plates in a low oven and prepare the Véronique Sauce, if you have not already done so.

Season both sides of each trout fillet with salt and pepper. Place a heavy 12-inch skillet (or use 2 smaller skillets; do not crowd the pan) over medium-high heat and add the butter. When the foam has subsided and the butter has just begun to turn brown, add the fillets and sear without moving for 1 minute. Carefully turn to the other side and sear for 1 minute more, then lower the heat to medium-low and continue cooking for 2 to 3 minutes more, until the fillets are firm and opaque through to the center. With a wide spatula, immediately transfer a fillet to each warm plate and spoon some of the sauce, with plenty of grapes, over the top. Serve at once.

Véronique Sauce

YIELD: 1-1/3 CUPS

3/4 cup clarified butter
4 shallots, very finely chopped
1/4 cup brandy
1 cup heavy cream
2 tablespoons Glacé de Viande or Veal Demi-glace (see page 205)
24 seedless red or green grapes
1 tablespoon granulated sugar
1 long, fireplace match

Place a sauté pan over medium-high heat and add the clarified butter. When it is hot, add and sauté the shallots for 30 seconds. Add the brandy and ignite with the match. When the flames die down, stir in the cream, Glacé de Viande, sugar, and the grapes. Bring to a boil, then lower the heat to medium-low and simmer briskly for about 2 minutes, until slightly thickened.

Shrimp and Scallops Eva

SERVES 4

To mold rice easily, line a small cup or ramekin with plastic wrap. Fill with rice firmly but without packing. Turn upside down onto the serving plate, and the rice will slip easily from the mold. Repeat for each serving.

1 pound medium, shell-on shrimp, peeled and deveined if necessary
  (if the vein is large and dark)
2 tablespoons olive oil
3/4 pound large sea scallops
1 small shallot, finely chopped
1-1/2 cups port wine
1 cup chicken stock (see page 204)
Pinch of saffron, lightly toasted and crushed
1 cup heavy cream
1/4 teaspoon freshly ground black pepper
1/4 teaspoon white pepper, preferably freshly ground
Kosher or sea salt (optional)
1/4 teaspoon Tabasco Sauce
1-1/2 to 2 cups cooked Jasmine or long grain rice
1-1/2 tablespoons finely chopped flat-leaf parsley, for garnish

Place a large sauté pan over high heat and add half of the olive oil.

Add and sauté the shrimp just until pink. With a slotted spoon, transfer to a platter and set aside. Add the scallops to the pan and sauté for about one minute, then remove from the pan.

Lower the heat to medium and add about 2 teaspoons more olive oil to the pan. Add the shallot and sauté for 2 minutes, until slightly softened. Stir in the port, chicken stock and the toasted saffron and increase the heat. Simmer the liquid for about 15 minutes, until reduced by about half. Stir in the cream and then reduce a little more if necessary, by simmering until the sauce coats the back of a spoon nicely.

Warm 4 dinner plates in a low oven.

Lower the heat so the sauce is barely simmering and stir in the shrimp, scallops and the black and white pepper. Taste for seasoning and adjust with a little salt, if necessary, and additional pepper, to taste. Simmer for 1 minute, just to heat the seafood through and remove from the heat.

For each serving, mold from 1/4 to 1/2 cup of the cooked rice in a small ramekin or bowl as described above, or use an ice cream scoop. Place a mound of the rice in the center of each plate and spoon the shrimp and scallop mixture around the rice. Sprinkle chopped parsley over the top and serve immediately.

Arnaud's Gulf Shrimp Papa Noel

SERVES 6

Each year Arnaud's celebrates a tradition from the mid-1800s, when Creole families gathered to share an elaborate meal after attending late Mass on Christmas Eve and New Years Eve. It is called a Réveillon dinner.

Three-Pepper Vinaigrette (recipe follows)
1 large or 2 small mirliton, peeled and cut into matchsticks
1-1/2 pounds (21 to 25-count) boiled Gulf shrimp (prepared with liquid or dry crab boil, see page 163)
2 small ripe avocados
2 cups spring mix (about 3 ounces) or other mixed baby lettuces
Small red onion, sliced very thinly and separated into rings, for garnish
Finely diced red, green and yellow peppers, for garnish

Prepare the dressing at least an hour before serving, to allow flavors to marry.

Bring a generous amount of water to a boil in a saucepan and place a bowl of iced water near the stove. Place the prepared mirliton in a basket or sieve and submerge in the boiling water for about 15 seconds.

Remove and plunge into the iced water, to stop the cooking. Spread on absorbent towels to dry briefly, then transfer to a bowl and drizzle with a spoonful of Three-Pepper Vinaigrette. Toss, and refrigerate until serving time.

Peel and devein the shrimp if necessary (if the vein is dark), leaving the tails on. Toss the lettuce with just enough dressing to coat the leaves lightly. Divide the salad among six small plates, placing it in the center, and top with some of the mirliton. Make a circle of shrimp around the salad, using 4 to 6 shrimp. Place a slice or two of avocado between the shrimp. Scatter with some of the red onion rings and a little of the diced pepper. Pass a small pitcher of Three-Pepper Vinaigrette at the table.

Three-Pepper Vinaigrette

YIELD: ABOUT 1-1/2 CUPS

1 large egg yolk
1/4 cup fresh lemon juice
1 cup extra virgin olive oil
1/4 cup vinegar
1/2 teaspoon very finely chopped shallot
1/4 teaspoon very finely chopped garlic
8 medium leaves basil, finely chopped
1/4 teaspoon coarsely ground black pepper
1/4 teaspoon Kosher or sea salt
2 tablespoons each finely chopped red, green and yellow bell pepper

In a small bowl, whisk together the egg yolk and 1 tablespoon of the lemon juice until smooth. Begin drizzling in the olive oil very slowly, whisking all the time, until an emulsion begins to form. Alternate adding the oil and vinegar until both are completely mixed in and emulsified. Whisk in the shallot, garlic, basil, pepper and salt. Fold in the diced peppers and taste for seasoning. Refrigerate until serving time.

Shrimp Clemenceau

SERVES 6

1/4 cup extra-virgin olive oil
2 pounds medium shrimp, peeled and deveined if necessary
    (if the vein is large and dark)
1 pound button mushrooms, wiped clean with a paper towel and quartered
1/4 cup (2 ounces, 1/2 stick) unsalted butter
1 small clove garlic, very finely chopped
1 small shallot, finely chopped
10 ounce package frozen green peas, thawed
Brabant potatoes, hot, for serving (recipe follows)
Kosher or sea salt and freshly ground black pepper
Six sprigs of flat leaf parsley, for garnish
Six thinly sliced rounds of lemon, for garnish

Place a serving platter and dinner plates in a low oven to warm.

Place a large skillet over medium-high heat and add the olive oil. When it is hot, add the shrimp and sauté, tossing occasionally, for 1-1/2 minutes. Add the quartered mushrooms and continue cooking for 1 minute more, then add the butter, garlic and shallot and cook for 1 more minute. Stir in the peas and season lightly with salt and pepper. Cook gently until the peas are tender and the mixture is hot, about 2 minutes more. Taste for seasoning and adjust if necessary, then add the Brabant potatoes and shake the pan to coat them evenly. Pour onto the serving platter, garnish with parsley and lemon slices and serve.

Brabant Potatoes

SERVES 6

2 pounds Idaho potatoes, washed, peeled and cut into 1/2-inch dice
2/3 cup vegetable oil, for frying
Kosher or sea salt and freshly ground black pepper
1-1/2 teaspoons finely chopped fresh herbs, such as oregano, thyme or rosemary
    (optional)

Heat the oven to its lowest setting and place a baking sheet lined with a doubled layer of paper towels inside.

In a large saucepan, bring 2 quarts water to a boil and add 1 tablespoon of salt. Add the diced potatoes and cook for 5 to 7 minutes, until just tender but not falling apart. Immediately drain in a colander and rinse with cool running water to stop the cooking. Shake the colander gently to remove excess water and pat dry thoroughly with paper towels.

Place a large skillet over high heat and add the oil. When it is hot, carefully add the potatoes cubes and fry without disturbing for 3 to 4 minutes, until golden. Toss and continue frying on the other side for 2 to 3 minutes more, until golden brown. With a slotted spoon, transfer the potatoes to the baking sheet and season lightly with salt and pepper and, if desired, chopped fresh herbs. Serve immediately, or keep warm for up to 5 minutes before adding to the Shrimp Clemenceau.

Crawfish Cardinale

To serve this dish as an appetizer, bake the mixture in individual ramekins at 350°, topping each with breadcrumbs and a sprinkle of paprika.

1 cup (8 ounces, 2 sticks) unsalted butter
Half a green pepper, stemmed, deeded, de-ribbed and finely chopped
2 stalks celery, finely chopped
3 green onions, green parts only, finely chopped
1 cup dry white wine
1/2 cup Shrimp Stock (see page 204) or clam juice
3 tablespoons all-purpose flour
Kosher or sea salt and freshly ground black pepper
2 cups heavy cream
1/4 cup tomato purée
1/4 teaspoon Cayenne pepper
1 tablespoon brandy or cognac
1 pound fresh, peeled crawfish tails
Hot, cooked pasta or rice, for serving

Warm 8 shallow bowls in a low oven and prepare the pasta or rice, if desired.

Place a large, heavy saucepan over medium-low heat and add the butter. When the foam subsides, add the green pepper, celery and green onions. Sauté, stirring occasionally, for about 5 minutes, or until the vegetables are softened. Add the wine and shrimp stock and bring to a boil over high heat. Boil for 5 to 6 minutes, until the liquid is reduced by about half.

In a medium bowl, mix the flour with a generous pinch of salt and pepper and then, with a fork, stir in 1 or 2 tablespoons of the cream to make a thick, smooth paste. Stir in the rest of the cream, then add the flour-cream mixture to the saucepan and stir until blended. Bring the mixture to a simmer and stir occasionally for a few minutes, until the sauce begins to thicken. Stir in the tomato purée, Cayenne and a generous pinch of salt. Continue cooking until the flour taste is gone, about 4 minutes. Stir in the brandy and, if the sauce is too thick, add a little more white wine. Taste for seasoning and correct if necessary. Remove the pan from the heat and gently stir in the crawfish tails. Return to the medium heat and stir gently for 2 minutes more, just to heat the crawfish through. Serve immediately, ladling over pasta or rice.

Coquilles Saint Jacques

Use a light hand in preparing this dish to avoid breaking the luscious morsels of tender crabmeat.

1/2 pound bay scallops, or sea scallops cut into bite-size pieces
1/2 pound jumbo lump crabmeat, picked over for bits of shell
Kosher or sea salt and white pepper
1/3 cup all-purpose flour
1 cup (8 tablespoons) butter
3 tablespoons finely chopped garlic
1/4 cup Herbsaint liqueur
2/3 cup green onions, white and green parts, finely chopped
2 fresh tomatoes, peeled, seeded and diced
1 cup buttered breadcrumbs
1 long, fireplace match

Season the scallops lightly with salt and white pepper. Season the crab lightly with salt and white pepper and sprinkle with the flour.

In a small bowl, use a fork to thoroughly combine 1 cup fresh breadcrumbs with 2 to 3 tablespoons of melted butter to moisten.

Melt the butter in a sauté pan over high heat, add the scallops and sear quickly, about 1 to 1-1/2 minutes. Remove from the pan and set aside. Add the garlic and sauté until softened but not browned. Add the crabmeat to the pan and toss for about 3 minutes, to cook the flour.

Return the scallops to the pan. Carefully pour off any remaining butter. Add the Herbsaint and flame, by lighting with the long match.

When the flames have burned out, reduce the heat to medium, add the green onions and tomatoes and cook for about 3 minutes, stirring occasionally.

Butter 6 scallop shells or small ovenproof dishes and place on a baking sheet. Divide the mixture evenly among the dishes and top each serving with buttered breadcrumbs. Place under the broiler until the crumbs are golden brown, 2 to 4 minutes. Serve immediately.

Shrimp-Stuffed Eggplant

SERVES 4 AS AN APPETIZER OR 2 AS AN ENTRÉE

Slice in half horizontally if serving to 4 guests.

1 large globe eggplant, stemmed and halved lengthwise
4 ounces (1/2 cup, 1 stick) unsalted butter
1/2 cup finely chopped parsley
1/2 cup diced green onion (white and green parts)
1/4 cup diced green pepper
1/2 teaspoon dried thyme
1 large clove garlic, very finely chopped
2 bay leaves
1 pound small to medium raw shrimp, peeled and deveined
1/2 cup chopped smoked ham (or use Andouille sausage, if available)
Kosher or sea salt
1/4 teaspoon Cayenne pepper
1/4 teaspoon white pepper
1/4 teaspoon freshly ground black pepper
1 teaspoon Tabasco
2 large eggs
1/2 cup dry white wine
About 1 cup fresh bread crumbs
2 tablespoons unsalted butter, cut into tiny pieces

In a large saucepan, bring a generous amount of lightly salted water to a boil. Add the eggplant halves and simmer until tender, 15 to 20 minutes. Drain cut sides down on paper towels until cool enough to handle. Carefully scoop out the inside pulp, leaving the shells intact and about 1/2-inch thick. Dice the pulp and set aside. If desired, sprinkle with salt to remove any bitterness.

In a large sauté pan or skillet, melt the butter over medium heat. Add the parsley, green onion, green pepper, thyme, garlic and bay leaves. Cook, stirring occasionally, until the vegetables are tender but not brown. Remove the bay leaves.

Add the shrimp and smoked ham and cook for 10 minutes, stirring occasionally. Season with salt to taste, the three peppers and Tabasco to taste (start with 1 teaspoon and work from there).

Add the diced eggplant to the pan and stir the mixture thoroughly. Cover and cook slowly for about 20 minutes, until very tender. Remove the pan from the heat and let cool to room temperature. In a small bowl, beat together the eggs and the white wine. Stir this mixture into the eggplant mixture until thoroughly blended, then stir in just enough of the fresh breadcrumbs to absorb the excess moisture. Reserve the remaining breadcrumbs for the topping.

Preheat the oven to 350°. Place the eggplant shells on a baking sheet and fill with the stuffing mixture. Sprinkle the tops with the remaining breadcrumbs and dot with little pieces of butter. Bake for 20 minutes, until tops are crisp and golden brown and serve.

Creole Crabcakes

SERVES 4

This mixture also makes a wonderful stuffing for shrimp or mushrooms.

1 tablespoon Creole mustard
1 large egg
1/2 cup mayonnaise
1 tablespoon fresh lemon juice
1/2 small red onion, finely chopped
1 green pepper, seeded, de-ribbed and finely chopped (or use 1/3 red, 1/3 yellow
    and 1/3 green peppers)
1 teaspoon finely chopped fresh cilantro
1 teaspoon Kosher or sea salt
1/2 teaspoon freshly ground black pepper
1 cup fine, dry breadcrumbs, plus more for the pan
1 pound lump crabmeat, picked over for bits of shell and cartilage
1/2 cup olive oil or clarified butter
1-1/2 cups Creole Sauce (see page 161)
1/4 cup Lemon Butter Sauce (see page 206), at room-temperature
4 sprigs of fresh basil, for garnish

If planning to cook the crab cakes right away, preheat oven to 375°.

In a large bowl, whisk together the mustard, egg, mayonnaise and lemon juice until smooth. Stir in the onions, green pepper, cilantro, salt and pepper. Gently but thoroughly fold in 3/4 cup of the breadcrumbs and the crabmeat. Place the remaining breadcrumbs in a shallow bowl.

With clean hands, portion out and form the crabmeat mixture into 16 round cakes, about 2 inches tall and 2 inches wide. Dredge each crab cake in the remaining breadcrumbs just to coat lightly and place on a platter.

If you plan to cook the crabcakes later, at this point you may cover them with plastic wrap, piercing the wrap in several places to prevent the cakes from getting soggy and refrigerate up to overnight.

Line a large baking sheet with parchment paper and dust lightly with breadcrumbs.

Place a large sauté pan over medium high heat and add the olive oil or clarified butter. Sauté the crabcakes in batches, for about 1 minute on each side, until golden brown. As they are finished, transfer to the prepared baking sheet. When all the crabcakes have been browned, finish cooking them in the hot oven for 5 minutes.

In a small saucepan, heat the Creole Sauce, then strain into another pan or a bowl.

For each serving, ladle a pool of Creole Sauce in the center of a hot dinner plate, and drizzle a little bit of Lemon Butter Sauce back and forth over the top. Place 4 crabcakes around the sauce, garnish with a sprig of basil and serve.

Crab Imperial

SERVES 6

This traditional dish is memorable for the lovely colors of the peppers, as well as the delicate crab flavor. If you prefer not to use, or do not have a pimiento handy, roast a small red pepper over flame until the skin is blackened and blistered, then place in a plastic or paper bag for 15 minutes to steam. Peel the charred skin away and chop.

1/2 cup (4 ounces, 1 stick) unsalted butter
1/2 cup finely chopped seeded and de-ribbed green pepper
1/2 cup grated onion
1/4 cup chopped pimiento
Kosher or sea salt and freshly ground black pepper
2 large eggs, lightly beaten
1/2 cup mayonnaise
1 tablespoon Creole mustard
1 pound lump crabmeat, picked over for bits of shell and cartilage

Preheat the oven to 350°. Butter six individual casseroles or scallop shells, or use prepared puff pastry cases. In a skillet, melt the butter over medium-low heat. Add the green pepper, onion and pimiento and cook until the pepper is soft, about 6 minutes. Season to taste with salt and pepper.

In a mixing bowl, use a fork to whisk together the beaten eggs, mayonnaise and Creole mustard. Stir in the cooked vegetables and then gently fold in the crabmeat, mixing gently so as not to break all the lumps apart.

Scoop into the casseroles, shells or pastry cases, place on a baking sheet and bake for 15 minutes. Let stand for about 2 minutes and serve.

Crab au Gratin

SERVES 4

This is a nice, simple, yet very rich dish.

3 tablespoons unsalted butter, plus extra for preparing the baking dishes
3 tablespoons all-purpose flour
1/2 teaspoon Kosher or sea salt
1/8 teaspoon ground white pepper
1/4 teaspoon paprika
1-1/2 cups heavy cream or half-and-half
1/2 cup grated medium-sharp Cheddar cheese
1 tablespoon Worcestershire sauce
8 ounces fresh crabmeat, picked over for bits of shell and cartilage
2 tablespoons dry sherry
1/2 cup fine, dry breadcrumbs, or crushed corn flakes

Preheat the oven to 400°.

Butter the base and sides of 4 small ovenproof dishes or ramekins. Place a saucepan over low heat and add the butter. When it has melted, stir in the flour, salt, pepper and paprika. Stir constantly until the mixture is smooth

Blend in the cream bit by bit, stirring frequently until the sauce is smooth and velvety.

Add the cheese, Worcestershire sauce and crabmeat and stir gently until the cheese melts. Remove from the heat and stir in the sherry. Scoop the mixture into the prepared dishes, top with an even coating of the bread crumbs and bake for 15 minutes or until golden brown. Let stand for 5 minutes (they will be very hot!) and serve.

Crab with Ravigote Sauce

SERVES 6

1 cup mayonnaise
1/3 cup Creole mustard
1/4 cup prepared horseradish, drained
1 green onion, white and light green parts only, very finely chopped
1 tablespoon finely chopped flat-leaf parsley
1 hard-cooked egg, finely chopped
1 tablespoon fresh lemon juice
1-1/2 teaspoons very finely chopped capers, plus extra whole capers for garnish
4 cups loosely packed mixed salad greens, cut into thin strips
1-1/2 pounds lump crabmeat, picked over for bits of shell and cartilage
1 whole lemon, cut into 6 wedges
Ravigote Sauce (see page 128)

Chill six appetizer plates in the refrigerator.

In a large bowl, combine the mayonnaise, mustard, horseradish, green onion, parsley, chopped egg, lemon juice and chopped capers. Mix together well.

To serve, place a mound of the shredded greens on each plate and top with a nice mound of crabmeat. Drizzle generously with the Ravigote Sauce and scatter a few whole capers around the plate. Garnish each salad with a lemon wedge and serve.

Crab Karen

SERVES 6

For appetizer-sized portions, cut the pastry into four-inch squares with a ravioli stamp or pizza wheel and fill with two tablespoon of crabmeat mixture.

3 green onions, white and green parts, finely chopped
3/4 cup Mushrooms Duxelles (see page 211)
2 large eggs
3/4 cup fine, dry breadcrumbs
2 teaspoons Kosher or sea salt
1/2 teaspoon ground white pepper
2 teaspoons fresh lemon juice
2 cups White Wine Sauce (see page 210)
1 pound lump crabmeat, picked over for bits of shell and cartilage
6 5-inch by 5-inch or very similar-size squares of puff pastry, either homemade or good quality frozen, thawed
Egg wash: 1 egg whisked with 1 tablespoon water

Preheat the oven to 350° and line a baking sheet with baking parchment.

In a large bowl, combine the green onions, duxelles, eggs, breadcrumbs, salt, pepper, lemon juice and 1/4 cup of the White Wine Sauce. Stir together until blended and then, using clean hands, gently mix in the crabmeat, taking care not to break up all of the lumps.

Place a sheet of pastry on a clean, lightly floured surface and brush lightly with egg wash. Spoon one-sixth of the crabmeat mixture in the top left corner corner, then fold the pastry over into a triangular shape, like an apple turnover, enclosing the crabmeat.

Seal the edges by pressing them together gently with a fork, and brush top of the parcel with more egg wash. Repeat the process to make six pastries and place on the baking sheet.

Bake until golden brown, 15 to 18 minutes. Warm the remaining White Wine Sauce over low heat. Ladle a nice pool of the sauce onto each serving plate, center a pastry over the sauce and serve.

Crawfish Napoleon with Ravigote Sauce

8 SERVINGS

Prepare the dressing and sauce early in the day or a day ahead of serving. In summer, this is a wonderful light entrée for dinner or special luncheon dish.

Champagne Vinaigrette (see page 91)
Napoleon Ravigote Sauce, recipe at right
2 cups spring mix or other mixed lettuces of your choice
3 avocados cut in lengthwise slices for garnish
Red pepper flakes for garnish
Frisee lettuce for garnish
16 slices ripe tomato, 1/2-inch thick (4-6 tomatoes, depending on size)
2 large eggs
2 tablespoons finely chopped flat-leaf parsley
3/4 cup all-purpose flour
2 cups dried breadcrumbs seasoned to taste with salt and pepper

Prepare the Champagne Vinaigrette and refrigerate. Just before serving, prepare the fried tomato slices as follows:

Prepare the Ravigote Sauce (at right) and refrigerate until serving.

Whisk the eggs in a small bowl. Place the flour in a pie tin or flat dish. Stir the seasoned breadcrumbs and parsley together in a small mixing bowl. Dredge the tomato slices in flour; shake off the excess. Dip each slice in the egg wash to coat lightly, then in the seasoned bread-crumbs. Place slices on a parchment-lined baking pan until all are ready to fry. Heat vegetable oil in deep fryer to 350 degrees. Fry the tomato slices a few at a time to avoid crowding until golden brown, approximately 45 seconds. As the slices cook, remove to drain on paper towels. Allow the oil to regain temperature between batches.

Toss the spring mix with half the Champagne Vinaigrette. Divide among 8 dinner plates. Center one slice fried tomato over the lettuce, spoon crawfish over, top with a second slice of tomato, more crawfish and a sprig of frisee lettuce to garnish. Garnish each serving with slices of avocado drizzled with Champagne Vinaigrette. Sprinkle red pepper flakes over the avocado.

Ravigote Sauce

4 cups precooked domestic crawfish tails
1/2 cup mayonnaise
1/4 cup Creole or other coarse grain mustard
2 tablespoons lemon juice
1 teaspoon Tabasco Sauce
1 teaspoon Worcestershire sauce
2 anchovies, finely minced
1 tablespoon capers
Kosher or sea salt and freshly ground black pepper to taste
1 tablespoon finely chopped fresh dill

Combine all ingredients, whisk well. Toss the cooked crawfish tails in the Ravigote Sauce and refrigerate until serving time.

Crawfish O'Connor

SERVES 4

Ralph S. O'Conner is a successful Houston entrepreneur, a close friend and one time partner of Casbarian. This is a richly flavored, robust dish, a standout, much like Ralph himself. Ralph is a table owner and a discreet brass plaque marks the O'Conner location in the main dining room.

Lobster or shrimp may be substituted for the crawfish.

3 tablespoon clarified butter (see page 206)
2 large shallots, finely chopped
1 pound fresh, peeled crawfish tails
1/2 teaspoon Kosher or sea salt
1/4 teaspoon freshly ground black pepper
2 cups Armoricaine sauce (see page 209)
2 cups cooked Jasmine rice, hot, for serving
1/4 cup finely chopped flat-leaf parsley, for garnish

Warm 4 shallow soup bowls in a low oven.

Place a large skillet over medium-high heat and add the clarified butter. When it is hot, add the shallots and stir for 30 seconds. Add the crawfish tails, salt and pepper and cook for 3 minutes, until pink.

Place about 1/2 cup of the cooked rice in the center of each warmed bowl and ladle the crawfish and sauce around the edges. Sprinkle generously with chopped parsley and serve.

Arnaud's extensive renovation went well over budget. The recession of the early 1980s and subsequent high interest rates placed Casbarian under considerable financial pressure. His creative solution was to sell tables. For $10,000, good customers, could have a plaque placed above a table that marked it as their own, in addition to other privileges of the house.

The personal-table concept not only brought in a significant amount of very welcome interest-free cash but also generated a bonus of national publicity.

Meat and Poultry

Many of the restored private dining rooms are named after the streets that surround Arnaud's. The connecting Iberville and Bienville rooms are ideal for pre-dinner gatherings, then dinner for up to 24 guests. As few as 14 or as many 60 guests can enjoy gala meals and receptions in these beautifully appointed rooms.

In addition to seafood, most dinner menus include a meat or poultry course. Arnaud's menu is designed to provide a comprehensive selection.

The centerpiece of many meals is a beef, veal or poultry entrée. The following recipes make a star turn on Arnaud's menu from time to time, rotating off and on as the seasons change.

Cornish Game Hen Whitecloud

SERVES 6

1/4 cup clarified butter (see page 206)
Wild Rice Stuffing (recipe follows)
1-1/2 cups Véronique Sauce (recipe follows), hot, for serving
Six tiny bunches of grapes (preferably Champagne
  grapes), for garnish
Sprigs of mint, for garnish

MARINADE

1/2 cup dry white wine
1/4 cup vegetable oil
1 small onion, coarsely chopped
4 cloves garlic, sliced
2 bay leaves
1 teaspoon black peppercorns
6 Cornish game hens, about 8 ounces each

STUFFING

1 cup wild rice
4 cups chicken stock (see page 204) or beef stock
  (see page 205)
5 tablespoons unsalted butter
1 white onion, finely chopped
4 ounces white mushrooms, finely chopped (about 1 cup)
1 cup drained and sliced water chestnuts
2 tablespoons finely chopped flat-leaf parsley
1 teaspoon dried sage
1/2 teaspoon Kosher or sea salt
1 teaspoon freshly ground black pepper

VÉRONIQUE SAUCE

3/4 cup clarified butter
4 shallots, very finely chopped
1/4 cup brandy
1 cup heavy cream
2 tablespoons Glacé de Viande or Veal Demi-glace
  (prepare your own as on page 205, or purchase from
  a specialty grocer)
24 seedless red grapes
1 tablespoon granulated sugar
1 long fireplace match

Please note that the wild rice stuffing takes over an hour to prepare.

In a baking dish large enough to snugly hold the hens in a single layer, combine and mix together the wine, vegetable oil, onion, garlic, bay leaves and peppercorns. Place the hens in the marinade and turn to coat all sides, making sure some of the marinade gets inside the cavities. Cover the dish with plastic wrap and refrigerate for at least 2 hours and up to 6 hours.

About 2 hours before you plan to serve, prepare the wild rice stuffing: In a colander, rinse the rice well under cold running water, sifting through it with your fingers. In a medium saucepan, bring the stock to a boil and slowly pour in the rice. Lower the heat to very low, cover the pan and simmer for 50 to 60 minutes, until the rice is tender. Drain in a colander, shaking to remove the excess moisture.

Preheat the oven to 375°.

Place a large skillet over medium heat and add the butter. When the foam has subsided, add and sauté the onions and mushrooms for about 5 minutes, until softened. Add the water chestnuts, parsley, sage, salt, pepper and cooked rice. Stir to mix and cook for 3 minutes to warm through. Remove from the heat, fluff with a fork, and keep warm.

Remove the birds from marinade and drain off the marinade from inside. Pat dry with paper towels and season liberally with salt and pepper.

Place a 10-inch sauté pan over medium-high heat and add the clarified butter. When the butter has just begun to smoke, add the hens and sauté skin-side down until golden brown, about 1-1/2 minutes on each side. With tongs (to avoid piercing the skin) transfer the hens to a roasting pan and cook for 30 to 35 minutes, until the juices at the thigh run clear when pierced with a small, sharp knife. Remove from the oven, let cool for 5 minutes, and, on a platter to save the stuffing, cut the hens in half lengthwise with poultry shears. Warm six plates in the turned-off oven.

To serve, place some of the stuffing in the center of the hot plates and place two hen halves on top of the rice. Spoon some of the Véronique Sauce, with plenty of grapes, around the hen. Garnish with a tiny bunch of grapes and a mint sprig.

VÉRONIQUE SAUCE

Place a sauté pan over medium-high heat and add the clarified butter. When it is hot, add and sauté the shallots for 30 seconds. Add the brandy and ignite with the match. When the flames die down, stir in the cream, Glacé de Viande, sugar and the grapes. Bring to a boil, then lower the heat to medium-low and simmer briskly for about 2 minutes, until slightly thickened.

Filet au Poivre

SERVES 6

Filet au Poivre is a beautifully seared filet, enhanced with fresh cracked pepper. A rich sauce completes the finish of bold tastes for beef lovers. It does not hold, so plan to serve it immediately after preparation.

6 (8 ounce) beef tenderloin filet steaks
6 tablespoons coarsely cracked black peppercorns
Kosher or sea salt
3 tablespoons clarified butter
3/4 cup brandy
3/4 cup heavy cream
1/2 cup Glacé de Viande or Veal Demi-glace (see page 205)
Half a bunch of fresh watercress, tough stems removed, for garnish

Season both sides of each filet with a little salt and cracked pepper, pressing the peppercorns into the meat firmly. Place a platter and six dinner plates in a low oven to warm.

Place a large sauté pan over high heat (or use two pans; on no account should you crowd the pan). Add the clarified butter and, when it is very hot, add the filets and brown without moving for 2 minutes. Turn and brown for 2 minutes, then reduce the heat to low and continue cooking for 6 minutes more for rare, 11 minutes more for medium-rare, 14 minutes more for medium, 16 minutes more for medium-well. Transfer the steaks to the platter in the oven and keep warm while you quickly finish the sauce.

Increase the heat to medium and deglaze the pan with the brandy, stirring and scraping all the delicious bits from the side of the pan. Add the cream and simmer, stirring, until the sauce is reduced to a coating consistency, about 2 minutes. Stir in the Glacé de Viande and cook for 1 minute more, to melt the Glacé. Taste for seasoning and adjust if necessary, then serve the steaks napped with several spoonfuls of the sauce. For an elegant presentation, slice and fan on the plate.

Filet Pot-au-Feu

The French translation literally means "a pot on the fire." It is a hearty dish, designed to be passed around the table While the ingredients may be removed following cooking and served individually, here we serve it as a main course and a soup all in one dish.

2 cups Veal Stock (see page 205)
Kosher or sea salt
4 whole black peppercorns
1 sprig fresh thyme
2 medium carrots, sliced 1/2-inch thick
3 leeks, white parts only, well washed and sliced
   1/2-inch thick
2 stalks celery, sliced 1/2-inch thick
4 red potatoes, washed and quartered
4 pieces beef tenderloin filet, about 4 ounces each
1/2 teaspoon freshly ground black pepper
4 slices bacon
1/4 cup olive oil
2 shallots, finely chopped
8 button mushrooms, brushed clean and quartered
1/2 pound hot Italian sausage, sliced 1/2-inch thick

In a medium saucepan combine the veal stock, 1/2 teaspoon of salt, the peppercorns, thyme, carrots, leeks, celery and potatoes. Bring to a boil over high heat, then lower the heat and simmer until the vegetables are just tender, about 8 minutes. Strain the stock into another pan, reserving the vegetables, and keep warm, covered, over very low heat.

Preheat the oven to 400° and place a rimmed baking sheet inside.

Season both sides of each filet with black pepper and a little salt, then wrap a slice of bacon around the outside rim of each filet, and secure it with a toothpick.

Place a large sauté pan over medium-high heat and add 2 tablespoons of the olive oil. When the oil is very hot but not smoking, place the filets in the pan to sear, without moving, for 1-1/2 minutes. Turn over and sear the other side for 1 minute, then transfer the filets to the baking sheet in the hot oven to finish cooking for 8 to 10 minutes, until done to your liking.

Place the pan in which you cooked the filets over medium heat and add the remaining olive oil. Sauté the shallots until translucent, about 4 minutes, then add the mushrooms and sauté, stirring, for about 2 minutes. Add the sausage slices and cook, stirring, for about 5 minutes more, until no longer pink. Do not allow the mixture to scorch. Add the reserved vegetables and cook for 1 minute, just to heat them through.

Remove the toothpicks from the meat and place a filet in the base of a shallow bowl. Divide the vegetable-sausage mixture among the bowls, on top of each filet and ladle the reserved warm broth over the top. Serve immediately.

Tournedos Grand Veneur

SERVES 6

1 tablespoon finely chopped flat-leaf parsley
1/4 teaspoon chopped fresh thyme or 1/2 teaspoon dried thyme
1 teaspoon coarsely cracked black peppercorns
6 tournedos of beef tenderloin filet, about 6 ounces each
2 tablespoons vegetable oil
1 tablespoon unsalted butter
1 small onion, finely chopped
3 cloves garlic, very finely chopped
Kosher or sea salt
Sauce Veneur (recipe at right) warm, for serving

In a small bowl, combine the parsley, thyme and peppercorns. Rub a pinch of the mixture into both sides of each tournedo. Place the tournedos on a platter, cover with plastic wrap and refrigerate for at least 2 and up to 5 hours. Remove from the refrigerator about 15 minutes before cooking.

Warm six dinner plates in a low oven.

Place a very large skillet over high heat and add the oil. When the oil is very hot but not smoking, add the butter, onion and garlic. The moment the butter melts, add the tournedos and cook without moving for 4 minutes; turn over and cook until only just done as desired, 2 to 4 minutes more. Transfer each tournedo to a warm plate, drizzle with some of the Sauce Veneur and serve.

Sauce Grand Veneur

MAKES ABOUT 1-1/4 CUPS

1 tablespoon vegetable oil
1 small onion, coarsely chopped
1 medium carrot, coarsely chopped
1 stalk celery, coarsely chopped
1/3 cup red wine vinegar
1 cup veal stock (see page 205)
1 cup venison stock or beef stock (see page 205)
1/4 cup finely chopped flat-leaf parsley
2 sprigs fresh thyme
1 bay leaf
1/4 cup heavy cream
2 tablespoons unsalted butter, cut into 4 pieces
1/4 cup red currants

Place a medium saucepan over high heat and add the oil. Add the onion, carrot and celery and cook, stirring frequently, until golden brown, about 5 minutes. Stir in the vinegar, then add the veal stock and venison stock. Bring to a simmer and add the parsley, thyme and bay leaf. Reduce the heat to very low, partially cover the pan, and simmer for 45 minutes, skimming occasionally to remove scum. Remove from the heat and strain into a small saucepan, pressing down on the solids to extract all their flavor. Place the reduced sauce over low heat and when it comes to a simmer, stir in the cream. Cook for 3 to 4 minutes, stirring occasionally, until the sauce thickens. Remove from the heat and whisk in the butter, whisking just until it has melted. Stir in the currants and keep warm until ready to serve.

Steak and Oyster Pie

SERVES 6

This is an old-fashioned Creole dish that is not often seen on a restaurant menu. It is more often prepared in home kitchens. The hearty beef and delicate oyster flavors compliment each other and hold their own together in the same pie. If desired, after the pie is baked the first time, you could let it come to room temperature, then cover and refrigerate overnight. Twenty minutes before serving, top with the well-thawed puff pastry and finish cooking as below, to reheat the filling and brown the pastry top.

3/4 pound beef tenderloin filet, cut into bite-size pieces
Kosher or sea salt and freshly ground black pepper
3 tablespoons (1-1/2 ounces) unsalted butter
1 pint oysters, drained and liquor reserved
1 cup Bordelaise Sauce (see page 207)
1/4 cup finely chopped flat-leaf parsley
9-inch unbaked pie shell, your own or purchased frozen and thawed
9-inch diameter circle of puff pastry dough, homemade or purchased frozen, and thawed

Preheat the oven to 375° and season the pieces of beef with salt and pepper.

Place a large skillet over medium-high heat and add the butter. When the foam subsides, add the beef and sear for about 30 seconds on each side, turning over with tongs. Using a slotted spoon, transfer the beef to a platter and set aside.

In the same pan, sauté the oysters quickly, just until the edges begin to curl (30 seconds to 1 minute only). Return the beef to the pan and stir in the Bordelaise sauce. Stir occasionally for 2 to 3 minutes, until the sauce is heated through. Taste for seasoning and correct as necessary. If the mixture is too thick, add 1 to 2 tablespoons of the reserved oyster liquor. Stir in the parsley and scoop the mixture into the unbaked pie shell. Bake for 35 to 40 minutes, until the filling is bubbling and the edges of the pastry are golden. Set the pie aside and increase the oven temperature to 400°.

Prick the puff pastry circle with a fork and carefully place on top of the filling.

Return the pie to the oven and bake for 12 to 15 minutes longer, until pastry is golden brown. Cool for 5 minutes, then use a sharp knife to cut the pie into wedges and serve.

Beef Brisket with Two Horseradish Sauces

SERVES 8

Madame Begue, one of New Orleans' original restaurateurs, is credited with popularizing this hearty dish. It is a local mainstay, especially in the winter months.

It is difficult to overcook this brisket; the longer it cooks, the more tender it becomes!

Bouquet Garni (see page 217), parsley stems and peppercorns doubled, and with the addition of 1/2 teaspoon coriander seeds
5 to 6 pounds beef brisket, trimmed
2 quarts beef stock (see page 205) or 2 quarts water with 1/2 cup prepared beef stock base
2 yellow onions, quartered
4 carrots, sliced 1-inch thick
2 leeks, washed well and sliced thick
2 stalks celery, sliced 1-inch thick
1 white cabbage, cut into 8 wedges
1 clove garlic, very finely chopped
White Horseradish Sauce (recipe follows), for serving
Red Horseradish Sauce (recipe follows), for serving

Tie the bouquet garni to one handle of a large pot. Place the brisket in the pot and add the beef stock and onions. Bring to a boil over high heat, then reduce the heat to low, cover and cook gently for about 4 hours, or until the meat can be cut with a fork. Remove from the heat and let stand covered for up to 2 hours before serving.

About 30 minutes before serving, preheat the oven to its lowest setting and place a platter and eight dinner plates inside to warm.

Place a large steamer basket over a large saucepan of simmering water and add the carrots. Cover the pan and steam the carrots until tender but not falling apart, about 12 minutes. Transfer to the platter, cover with aluminum foil and keep warm in the oven. Add the leeks and celery to the steamer and again, steam until tender, 8 to 10 minutes. Transfer to the platter and steam the cabbage wedges for 15 minutes, until tender.

While the cabbage is steaming, reheat the brisket slightly, if necessary.

To serve: Transfer the brisket to a cutting board or serving platter and trim off any remaining fat. Cut into 1/4-inch slices and serve on warm plates, with an assortment of the steamed vegetables and a wedge of cabbage. Ladle a little broth over each serving, just to moisten the meat and pass the two Horseradish Sauces at the table.

White Horseradish Sauce

2 cups heavy cream
5 tablespoons prepared horseradish
1 tablespoon Kosher or sea salt, or to taste
1 teaspoon coarsely cracked black pepper

In a large bowl, beat the cream until stiff peaks form. Fold in the horseradish, salt and pepper. Refrigerate for at least one hour before serving, for the flavors to blend.

Red Horseradish Sauce

1 cup ketchup
5 tablespoons prepared horseradish
1 tablespoon Kosher or sea salt
1 tablespoon freshly ground black pepper

In a bowl, stir together all the ingredients with a fork. Chill, covered, until serving time. Refrigerate for at least one hour before serving, for the flavors to blend.

Veal Charlemond

Serves 6

6 slices of veal tenderloin, about 3/4-inch thick, patted dry with paper towels
Kosher or sea salt and freshly ground black pepper
1/4 cup clarified butter (see page 206)
Charlemond Sauce (recipe follows), hot, for serving
Risotto of your choice, for serving (optional)

Preheat the oven to its lowest setting and place a platter and six dinner plates inside to warm.

Season both sides of each piece of veal with salt and pepper. Place a large skillet over medium-high heat and add the clarified butter. When it is very hot, add 3 of the veal slices to the pan and sear for 2 minutes, until slightly golden. Turn to the other side and sear for 2 minutes more, until firm. Transfer to the platter in the warm oven and cook the remaining 3 slices of veal in the same way.

To serve: Make a pool of Charlemond Sauce on each plate and center a slice of veal over the top. If desired, serve risotto on the side.

Charlemond Sauce

Yield: About 1-1/2 cups

1 tablespoon unsalted butter
1 small shallot, very finely chopped
3 green onions, white and light green parts only, finely chopped
1/4 pound sliced white mushrooms
1 Bouquet Garni (see page 217)
1 small clove garlic, very finely chopped
1/2 cup dry white wine
Blond Roux made with 2 tablespoons butter and 2 tablespoons flour (see page 216)
Kosher or sea salt and white pepper, preferably freshly ground
1 cup heavy cream
1/2 teaspoon granulated chicken bouillon (optional)

Place a large saucepan over medium heat and add the butter. When the foam begins to subside, add the shallot and green onions and cook, stirring occasionally, until softened and translucent, 5 to 6 minutes. Add the mushrooms and cook for 3 minutes more, until tender.

Add the bouquet garni, garlic and white wine and bring to a simmer. Cook until the wine has reduced by about half and the mixture is slightly juicy. Strain the liquid into a clean saucepan and set aside, reserving the shallot-mushroom mixture in the strainer separately. Discard the bouquet garni.

In a small pan, make the Roux as directed on page 216. Cook until thick, but not at all brown.

Add the cream and the chicken bouillon, if using, to the reduced wine, then use a whisk to blend in the Roux until smooth. Season with a pinch each of salt and pepper. Bring to a boil over medium heat and cook, stirring occasionally, until thickened. Return the mushrooms and onions to the sauce. Taste for seasoning and adjust as necessary. Lower heat to very low and simmer the sauce partially covered for 4 to 5 minutes, to marry the flavors.

Veal Chantale

SERVES 4

8 (3 ounce) pieces of veal tenderloin, about 1/2-inch thick
Kosher or sea salt and freshly ground black pepper
4 tablespoons (2 ounces, 1/2 stick) unsalted butter
Chantale Sauce (recipe follows, may be prepared in advance), warmed
1 lemon, ends trimmed and thinly sliced, for serving
4 sprigs flat-leaf or curly parsley, for serving

Warm 4 plates or a serving platter in a low oven.

Season the tenderloins on both sides with salt and pepper. Place a very large skillet (or use two skillets; avoid overcrowding at all costs) over medium-high heat and add the butter. When the foam subsides and the butter has just begun to brown, add the veal and sear for about two minutes on each side for medium-rare, 2-1/2 minutes per side for medium (longer cooking is not recommended).

Transfer two tenderloins to each of the plates, or arrange all the veal on a platter. Garnish with a few lemon slices and parsley sprigs. Ladle about 1/4 cup of the Chantale Sauce over each serving and pass the remaining sauce at the table.

Chantale Sauce

YIELD: 1-1/2 CUPS

1/2 cup clarified butter (see page 206)
1 cup sliced mushrooms (use a mixture of shiitake, oyster, button or any
    mushrooms available)
1 small shallot, very finely chopped
1/3 cup dry white wine
1-1/2 cups heavy cream
2 tablespoons Glacé de Viande or Veal Demi-glace (see page 205)
1/2 teaspoon Kosher or sea salt
1/4 teaspoon white pepper, preferably freshly ground
1 teaspoon fresh lemon juice

Place a large skillet over medium heat and add the clarified butter. When it is hot, add the sliced mushrooms and sauté for 4 minutes, stirring, until tender. Add the shallot and sauté for 1 minute more. Add the wine, adjust the heat so the mixture simmers and reduce by about half (this will take from 3 to 4 minutes). Stir in the cream, bring the mixture to a boil and stir in the Glacé de Viande, salt and pepper. Lower the heat and again simmer to reduce by about half, about 10 minutes. Add the lemon juice and cook for 2 minutes more. Use immediately or cool to room temperature and refrigerate overnight. Warm gently in the top of a double boiler before serving.

Panéed Veal Victoria

SERVES 4

Panéed Veal Victoria is named for Jane's sister Vickie Moat. The dish is rooted in New Orleans' Italian heritage and is most often served partnered with a creamy Pasta Alfredo or Pasta Primavera

1-1/2 to 2 pounds of veal round, cut into 3/8-inch slices
Kosher or sea salt and freshly ground black pepper
1 large egg, beaten with 3 tablespoons cold water
Seasoned, dry breadcrumbs, for coating (about 1 cup)
Vegetable oil, for deep frying
Lemon wedges, for serving

Place each veal cutlet between 2 sheets of plastic wrap and use the scored side of a meat mallet to pound out to an even thickness, about 1/4 inch. Repeat with the remaining pieces of veal. Place a sheet of baking parchment on a large baking sheet. Place the egg mixture in one wide, shallow bowl and the breadcrumbs in another.

Season both sides of each pounded cutlet with salt and pepper, then the dip the pieces of veal in the egg and water mixture and then in the seasoned breadcrumbs. Take care to coat each piece thoroughly with crumbs; then very gently shake off the excess. Place the coated pieces of veal on the parchment and let dry for 10 minutes.

Preheat the oven to its lowest setting and place a platter lined with a double layer of paper towels and four dinner plates inside.

In an electric deep fryer, or a large heavy pot no more than half filled with oil, heat the oil to 375°. Gently lower 2 pieces of veal into the hot oil and fry until golden brown, nudging occasionally, about 4 minutes. Retrieve with a skimmer and transfer to the platter in the oven while you fry the remaining pieces of veal in the same way. Serve very hot, on the hot plates, with lemon wedges on the side.

Calves Liver Robichaux

SERVES 4

Danny Robichaux, Arnaud's long-time private dining director, is an Orleanian with an old French surname. He ensures that events in his keeping are flawless.

Included here are recipes for the special mashed potatoes and braised red cabbage that traditionally accompany this dish at Arnaud's.

8 slices bacon
1/4 cup clarified butter (see page 206), for the onions
2 yellow onions, quartered and thinly sliced
1 cup all-purpose flour
1-1/2 teaspoons Kosher or sea salt
1 teaspoon white pepper, preferably freshly ground
4 slices calves liver, about 3/8-inch thick and 6 ounces each
2 tablespoons clarified butter (see page 206)
1/2 cup dry white wine
4 tablespoons cold Garlic Butter (see page 206), cut into 4 pieces
Mashed Potatoes and Braised Red Cabbage (recipes follow), optional, for serving

In a large skillet, fry the bacon until crisp. Drain on paper towels and set the bacon and the pan aside, leaving the bacon fat in the pan. Use the pan to cook the Braised Cabbage as directed at right. Prepare the Mashed Potatoes as directed at right.

Warm four dinner plates in a low oven.

Place a medium skillet over medium heat and add the clarified butter. When it is hot, add the onions and cook, tossing occasionally so that they brown evenly, for about 5 minutes. Remove the pan from the heat, cover and keep warm until serving time.

In a shallow bowl, combine the flour, salt and pepper and blend well. Pull any threads away from the liver. Place a large sauté pan over medium heat and add the clarified butter. Dredge the liver slices in the seasoned flour, shaking off any excess. When the butter is very hot, add all the liver to the pan and sauté without moving for 2 minutes. Turn over and cook for 2 minutes more.

Add the white wine and stir to deglaze the pan for 1 minute. Add the cold Garlic Butter and swirl the pan until the butter has just melted and the sauce coats the liver nicely.

Place a slice of liver on each warm plate and ladle one or two generous spoonfuls of sauce over the top. Top each with 2 slices of bacon and some of the caramelized onions. Spoon a nice mound of mashed potatoes and braised cabbage onto each plate, sprinkle a little parsley onto the mashed potatoes and serve at once.

Braised Red Cabbage

SERVES 4

Half a yellow onion, coarsely chopped
1 small red cabbage, damaged outer leaves removed, quartered, cored and cut into
    thin slices (julienne)
1 clove garlic, very finely chopped
2 tablespoons dry white wine
1 tablespoon honey

Preheat the oven to 450°.

In the pan that was used to cook the bacon, heat the reserved fat over medium-high heat. When the fat is hot, add the onion and sauté for 2 minutes, stirring occasionally. Add the cabbage and sauté for 3 minutes, then add the garlic, wine and honey. Sauté, stirring, for 3 minutes more, then cover the pan and bake for 20 minutes, until tender. Serve hot.

Mashed Potatoes

SERVES 4

5 large Idaho potatoes (about 1-3/4 pounds), peeled and quartered
1/2 cup (4 ounces, 1 stick) unsalted butter, at room temperature
3 ounces cream cheese, at room temperature
1 cup whole milk, at room temperature, plus a little more if necessary
1-1/2 teaspoons Kosher or sea salt
1-1/2 teaspoons white pepper, preferably freshly ground

Preheat the oven to its lowest setting and place the bowl of an electric stand mixer inside to warm.

In the top of a large double boiler set over simmering water, steam the potatoes until tender, 20 to 25 minutes (check occasionally to be sure the water does not boil away). Transfer the potatoes to the warm mixing bowl and add the remaining ingredients. Using the paddle attachment of the stand mixer, mix at medium speed until the mixture is smooth and creamy, about 5 minutes. If the mixture is too thick, add a tablespoon or 2 of milk to thin. Serve at once, or cover with aluminum foil and keep warm in the oven until serving time.

Grilled Pork Loin with Braised Red Cabbage and Wild Mushrooms

SERVES 4

New Orleans' mild winters still stimulate appetites for more substantial entrées. This savory dish also includes apples, completing a well-rounded treat for chilly evenings.

1/2 cup (4 ounces, 1 stick) unsalted butter
1 cup sliced fresh shiitake mushrooms
1 cup sliced cremini or white mushrooms
Kosher or sea salt and freshly ground black pepper
1 medium cooking apple, peeled, cored and cut into 1/4-inch dice
1 medium onion, coarsely chopped
Half a medium red cabbage, quartered, cored and shredded
3/4 cup apple juice
8 center-cut pork loin medallions, about 4 ounces each
Vegetable oil, for brushing

Place a skillet over medium-high heat and add 2 tablespoons (1 ounce) of the butter. When the foam has subsided, add the sliced shiitake and cremini mushrooms and cook, stirring, for about 5 minutes, until almost tender. Season with salt and pepper and set the pan aside.

Place another skillet over medium heat and add the remaining 3 ounces of butter. When the foam has subsided, add the apple and onion and cook, stirring, for about 10 minutes, until the onions are translucent. Add the cabbage and reduce the heat to low. Cover the pan and cook for 2 minutes. Add the apple juice and simmer, partially covered, for 3 minutes more, until juicy and tender. Season to taste with salt and pepper and set the pan side.

Warm the dinner plates in a low oven and prepare a grill for medium-high heat cooking.

Brush both sides of the pork medallions with a little vegetable oil and season with salt and pepper. Grill for 4 to 5 minutes on each side, until firm and cooked through to the center.

Place a mound of cabbage in the center of each plate and lean two pieces of pork up against it. Place the mushrooms around the pork and serve.

Stuffed Quail au Chambertin

Serves 6

The Bordelaise Sauce may be made ahead of time and need not be warm when you begin preparing this dish.

12 boneless quail, patted dry with paper towels
1-1/2 cups Bordelaise Sauce (see page 207)
1/4 cup Chambertin or other red Burgundy wine
2 tablespoons unsalted butter
3 cups sliced white or cremini mushrooms
1/4 cup finely chopped flat-leaf parsley

STUFFING

8 ounces lean pork loin, cut into 1/2 inch cubes
10 ounces veal, from the shank, cut into 1/2-inch cubes
5 ounces chicken livers
2 shallots, very finely chopped
1/2 teaspoon white pepper, preferably freshly ground
1/2 teaspoon freshly ground black pepper
1/2 teaspoon Kosher or sea salt
1/2 teaspoon ground allspice
2 tablespoons finely chopped flat-leaf parsley
1 large egg, lightly beaten
2 tablespoons heavy cream
2 tablespoon port

First, make the stuffing: Chill the cubes of meat and the chicken livers for 30 minutes. Place in a food processor and pulse into a smooth paste. Transfer to a large bowl and add the shallots, white and black pepper, salt, allspice, parsley, egg, cream and port. With a fork, blend until all the ingredients are evenly distributed. If desired, cover and refrigerate for up to 2 hours before stuffing the quail.

Preheat the oven to 400°. Stuff each quail with about 1/4 cup of stuffing and place breast side up in the roasting pan. Mix 2 tablespoons of the Bordelaise Sauce with the Chambertin wine and add the mixture to the pan. Cover securely with aluminum foil and bake for 20 minutes.

While the quail are roasting, sauté the mushrooms in the butter for about 5 minutes, until tender.

Transfer the quail to a platter, tent with foil, and place in the turned-off oven to keep warm. Put six dinner plates in the oven to warm.

Pour the juices from the roasting pan into a small saucepan and place over high heat. Simmer the sauce until it has reduced to about one third of its volume, about 4 minutes.

Stir in the remaining Bordelaise Sauce and the sautéed mushrooms, bring to a boil, then reduce the heat and simmer gently for about 3 minutes. Place two quail on each plate, spoon some of the sauce over the top and sprinkle with chopped parsley.

Chicken Bonne Femme with Brabant Potatoes

SERVES 4

In this dish, the chickens may be pan-sautéed or oven-roasted, either version works fine. If you choose to pan-sauté, you will have to wait until the chickens are cooked to prepare the onions.

2 whole chickens, rinsed well, patted dry, halved lengthwise, and backbones removed with poultry shears (have your butcher do this if desired)
Kosher or sea salt and freshly ground black pepper
Vegetable oil, for frying
2 large onions, cut into 1/4-inch slices
3 cloves garlic, very finely chopped
Brabant Potatoes (see page 122), hot, for securing

FOR PAN-SAUTÉED CHICKENS

Preheat the oven to its lowest setting and place four dinner plates inside to warm.

Season all sides of the chicken halves generously with salt and pepper. Place a large skillet over medium heat and add 1 tablespoon of vegetable oil. When the oil is very hot but not smoking, add two chicken halves, skin side down, to the pan and sauté for about 10 minutes, regulating the heat so the chicken sizzles but does not burn. Turn over and brown the other side, 10 to 15 minutes more. The chicken should be cooked all the way through. Transfer to a paper towel-lined baking sheet and keep warm in the oven while you cook the remaining chicken halves in the same way. (If the drippings in the pan burn, discard them, wipe the pan with a paper towel and begin with fresh oil.)

FOR OVEN-ROASTED CHICKENS

Preheat the oven to 350°. Generously salt and pepper both sides of each chicken half. Place the chicken halves on racks in one large or two medium roasting pan(s). Roast for 20 to 25 minutes, until the juices near the thigh run clear when pierced with a small, sharp knife.

TO SERVE

If you have sautéed the chickens, use the same pan to cook the onions, wiping it with a towel and adding fresh oil if necessary. Place the pan over low heat, add the onions and sauté for about 15 minutes, until they are softened and slightly golden. Add the garlic and cook, stirring, for two minutes more. If you have oven-roasted the chickens, use a clean pan to brown the onions as directed.

Place a chicken half in the center of each plate and divide the potatoes among the plates, surrounding the chicken. Spoon the onions over the top and serve at once.

Chicken Pontalba

SERVES 4

The Baroness Pontalba was a strong and colorful woman of her time. In 1840, she constructed the first apartment buildings in America. The twin red brick structures face each other across Jackson Square in the French Quarter. There lace wrought iron balconies feature swirling initials "AP" as part of their pattern. The street level continues to be retail space, as designed, while the second and third stories are coveted apartments.

1/2 cup (4 ounces, 1 stick) lightly salted butter
1 medium onion, finely chopped
12 green onions, white and light green parts only, thinly sliced
1 clove garlic, very finely chopped
2 white potatoes (not Idaho), about 1-1/2 pounds, peeled and cut into 1/2-inch cubes
4 ounces lean ham, cut into 1/4-inch dice
4 ounces white or cremini mushrooms, brushed clean and sliced
1/2 cup dry white wine
1 tablespoon finely chopped flat-leaf parsley
1 cup all-purpose flour
1 teaspoon Kosher or sea salt
1/2 teaspoon freshly ground black pepper
1/8 teaspoon Cayenne
2 pounds boneless chicken breasts, legs, and thighs (about two whole, small fryers)
1 cup vegetable oil
2 cups Béarnaise Sauce (see page 207), hot, for serving

Preheat the oven to 200°.

Place a heavy, 12-inch sauté pan or deep skillet over medium-low heat and add the butter. When the foam has subsided, add the onion, green onions, garlic and potatoes and cook over low heat until the vegetables are browned, about 15 minutes, stirring frequently. Add the diced ham, mushrooms, wine and parsley and cook for 8 minutes more, stirring occasionally, until the wine is reduced and the potatoes are fork-tender. Remove the pan from the heat and use a slotted spoon to transfer all the vegetables and ham to a large gratin dish attractive enough to bring to the table; allow the excess butter to drain back into the pan. Bake the vegetable mixture, covered, until the chicken is cooked (at this low temperature, 10 minutes either way won't make much difference).

If desired, cool the vegetable mixture to room temperature and refrigerate overnight before reheating and proceeding with the recipe.

In a wide, shallow bowl, combine and mix together the flour, salt, black pepper and Cayenne. Cut up the larger pieces of boneless chicken, so that none are thicker than about 1/2 inch, or longer than about 1-1/2 inches.

Dredge the pieces of chicken in the seasoned flour, gently shaking off the excess. Add the vegetable oil to the butter in the original pan and place the pan over medium-high heat. When the oil and butter mixture sizzles gently, add and fry the chicken pieces until cooked through and golden brown, about 10 minutes. Turn frequently with tongs to brown evenly. Remove the chicken, drain for a minute on a paper towel-lined platter and arrange evenly over the vegetables.

Return the dish to the oven while you prepare the Béarnaise Sauce, if you have not already done so. To serve, spoon the sauce evenly over the entire surface and bring to the table.

Chicken Rochambeau

SERVES 6

Two of New Orleans' favorite sauces are featured in this recipe. For the supreme impact on the taste-buds, the Bordelaise and Béarnaise should remain separate until the first forkful. It's best to make the Béarnaise just before serving; the Bordelaise may be made one day ahead.

3 cups hot Bordelaise Sauce (see page 207; may be prepared ahead)
1-1/2 cups hot Béarnaise Sauce (see page 207)
6 boneless, skinless chicken breasts (5 to 6 ounces each, see Note below)
1/2 cup dry white wine
4 shallots, finely chopped
Six 1/2-inch thick slices of wide French bread, toasted
6 slices Canadian bacon, sautéed in 1 tablespoon butter until crisp

Preheat the oven to 350°. Prepare the two sauces, if you have not already done so and keep warm in two double boilers, over barely simmering water.

Place the chicken breasts in a large, ovenproof saucepan or Dutch oven and add just enough water to barely cover them. Add the wine and shallots and place the pan over high heat. Bring the liquid just to a simmer and then transfer the pan to the oven. Cover the pan and cook for 8 to 10 minutes, until the chicken is firm and opaque through to the center. Lift from the poaching liquid with a skimmer.

Ladle about 1/2 cup of the Bordelaise Sauce onto the center of each dinner plate. Center a slice of bread in each pool of sauce and cover with a slice of crisped Canadian bacon. Place a chicken breast on top of the bacon and ladle about 1/4 cup of the Béarnaise sauce over each. Serve immediately.

Note: For a special presentation, curl a raw chicken breast inside each of six heatproof 4 or 5 ounce ramekins and place in the skillet right side up before adding the poaching liquid. Poaching liquid should cover the rims of the ramekins by 1/2-inch. The poached breasts will be perfectly shaped to fit on top of the bread.

Leading into the Jazz Bistro and Richelieu Bar is an intricate mosaic floor. The patterns change throughout the restaurant and indicates the various original buildings.

Duck Ellen in Blueberry Sauce

Serves 4

Named in honor of Casbarian's mother, Ellen, this is an involved recipe and worth doing for a special occasion. For a far easier variation, make the duck breasts only, without the stuffed legs. Use a chicken carcass to enrich the veal stock for the sauce.

Ellen immediately took over housekeeping, initiating a reign of terror in the kitchen and commanding her large staff to meet exacting standards of cleanliness. Her green thumb is evident through all of the dining rooms where lush plants enliven the elegant spaces and flourish under her care.

2 plump, fresh ducklings, with their giblets
1 onion, coarsely chopped
1 carrot, coarsely chopped
2 cups Veal Stock (see page 205)
1/4 cup port, for deglazing the pan
4 ounces veal shoulder, chopped and chilled until very cold
4 ounces pork tenderloin, chopped and chilled until very cold
1 large egg, lightly beaten
Kosher or sea salt and freshly ground black pepper
1/4 cup cognac
1/4 cup port, for making the sauce
1/4 cup granulated sugar
1/4 cup water
1/4 cup red wine vinegar
1 pint blueberries, washed several blueberries reserved for garnish
2 tablespoons peanut oil

Preheat the oven to 400°.

Remove the giblets from the ducks and set them aside in the refrigerator. Cut off the legs and thighs from each duck in one piece (you will have four leg-thigh joints). Refrigerate until after you make the duck stock and the meat stuffing.

With a sharp knife, working as close to the bones as possible, remove the breasts in two pieces from each duck. Refrigerate the four breasts until just before serving time.

With a heavy cleaver, chop the duck carcasses into 2- or 3-inch pieces and place in a roasting pan with the onion and carrot. Toss together and roast for 45 minutes, toss with tongs once or twice, until nicely browned. Transfer the bones and vegetables to a large pot and add the veal stock. Add the port to the roasting pan and deglaze, stirring up all the delicious bits from the base and sides of the pan. Add the deglazing liquid to the pot and bring to a boil over high heat. Lower the heat and simmer very gently, partially covered, for at least one hour, preferably two.

In a food processor, combine the reserved livers and gizzards with the chilled veal and pork. Purée for about 30 seconds, scraping down the sides of the bowl, and add the egg. Season with a large pinch each of salt and pepper and continue to process to a smooth purée. Add the cognac and port and blend until smooth.

Preheat the oven to 375°.

With a very sharp knife, cut open the duck leg pieces from the back, all the way from top to bottom, and remove the bones. Always keep the knife scraping against the bone to be sure you don't leave behind too much of the meat. Fill the resulting pockets with the meat purée and fold the skin around it to enclose. Secure with toothpicks or cooking twine.

Butter four 8- or 9-inch pieces of aluminum foil and wrap a duck leg in each one to make a firm package. Place the packages on a rimmed baking sheet and roast for 60 to 75 minutes, until the internal temperature reaches 165° on a meat thermometer. Warm four plates in the turned-off oven.

While the legs are roasting, make the sauce in a large, heavy saucepan. Stir together the sugar and water and, over high heat, cook the liquid, stirring at first until the sugar dissolves, to a medium-dark, syrupy caramel. As soon as the caramel is brown, stand back and add the vinegar (it will splatter). Add the blueberries and continue cooking until thick and syrupy, about 5 minutes.

Strain the duck stock into the caramel mixture, pressing down on the solids to extract all the juices. Stir together and simmer for 5 minutes to marry the flavors. Keep warm, covered.

Place a large skillet over high heat and add the peanut oil. When it is very hot but not smoking, add the duck breasts skin side down and cook for 1 minute. Remove from pan and remove the skin from the breasts (see Note below). Return the skinless duck breasts to the pan and sauté for 3 to 4 minutes per side, until firm and only just slightly pink at the center, or to taste.

Slice each duck breast into 1/4-inch slices and fan out on each plate opposite the unwrapped, stuffed legs and a generous spoonful of the blueberry sauce.

Note: If you cannot bear to discard the duck skin, cover and refrigerate for up to 24 hours before making duck cracklings as follows (use as a topping for salad): Cut the skin into 1/4-inch strips crosswise and sauté in a large, dry skillet over low heat for 15 to 20 minutes, turning occasionally, until very crisp (the skin will render a great deal of fat, which may be saved for sautéed potatoes). Retrieve with a slotted spoon and drain on paper towels. Scatter over a dressed green salad just before serving.

The Casual Side of Creole Cooking

While Orleanians dine extravagantly on occasion, we also relish a great plate of red beans and rice, jambalaya, gumbo, fresh seafood and other more casual concoctions stirred up in local kitchens. Rice is a staple in these dishes; many are served for large gatherings.

It is this kind of Creole pot food cooking that we all enjoy at home. In 1994 Casbarian converted a building at the end of his properties on Bourbon Street. It is named Remoulade, in honor of Arnaud's sauce and is a café serving a food festival with the best of New Orleans home cooking and fresh seafood. It includes an oyster bar and stands as his nod to casual Creole fare. As lagniappe (a little something extra, say *lan-yap*) Remoulade offers a few of its big sister's specialties such as Oysters Arnaud and Shrimp Arnaud.

The property has a very long history. In 1722, four years after the city's founding, it was identified on the de la Tour map (see page 220). On January 14, 1795, Don Jorge Inguenberty sold it to Luis Duval, and the transfer of ownership notes, "A house and kitchen exists on this land."

It did then and it does now.

Remoulade features a handsome antique oyster bar and celebrates fresh Louisiana seafood along with a fine selection of local favorites.

Red Beans and Rice

SERVES A CROWD

This recipe is subject to as many interpretations as there are Creole cooks. Some cooks soak the beans overnight, some do not soak at all. Soaking rids the beans of that unfortunate extra kick that can give sensitive digestive tracts a problem.

NOTE: Red beans and rice are also served with fried chicken or pork chops.

RAPID-SOAK METHOD:
Forget to soak those beans overnight? Cover with cold water and bring to a rapid boil. Boil for 5 minutes, then turn off the heat, cover, and let stand for one hour. Rinse thoroughly with cold water (change the water two or three times) and proceed with the recipe.

2 pounds (four cups) dried red beans, soaked overnight or rapid-soaked as above

2 smoked ham hocks

1 bottle Abita Amber beer, or other local style beer (optional)

1 white or yellow onion, chopped (about 2 cups)

1 green pepper, stemmed, seeded and de-ribbed and chopped

2 stalks celery, chopped

1/2 cup chopped parsley

10 cloves garlic, very finely chopped

2 tablespoons Worcestershire sauce

1 teaspoon dried oregano

2 teaspoons dried thyme

4 bay leaves

3-inch stick cinnamon (optional)

1 teaspoon freshly ground black pepper

1 teaspoon ground white pepper

1/2 teaspoon Cayenne pepper

2 (2-inch) pieces salt pork, blanched for 5 minutes in boiling water

1 pound smoked sausage, such as andouille or Kielbasa, cut into 3-inch lengths

Cooked white rice, for serving

In a large stock pot, combine the prepared beans, ham hocks, beer, vegetables, all the seasonings, salt pork and sausage. Add one gallon of water (be sure the water covers the beans by at least 2 inches). Place over high heat and bring the water to a boil. Reduce the heat and simmer, partially covered, for 3 hours. Remove the cinnamon stick and ham hocks.

When the hocks are cool enough to handle, pick off the meat and return it to the pot. Discard the skin and bones. Return to the pot and simmer for about 1 hour more, until the beans begin to break down. If desired, reduce the heat to very, very low and simmer for another hour, for a total of 5 hours. For the best flavor, cool to room temperature, cover, and refrigerate overnight. Remove one cup of beans and mash; return them to the pot. To serve, warm through over low heat, stirring occasionally. If the beans seem too thick, thin with water or chicken stock to the desired consistency. Ladle over white rice.

Monday in New Orleans is to red beans and laundry as baked beans and laundry is to Monday in Boston: tradition. Across town red beans and rice are served for lunch and dinner alongside fried chicken, hot sausage or pork chops, simmered with ham bones and slow cooked for hours. Red beans also make a rich soup by simply adding chicken stock then topping the hot soup with finely chopped onion and shredded cheddar cheese. Red beans also create an especially delicious omelette. Please see page 100.

Meat Pies came to special attention at the Jazz Fest food booths. They are a popular eat-in-hand snack for wandering around the music stages.

Meat Pies

YIELD: 12 PIES

If you are hungry for a meat pie and don't have much time, try this easy version for a great hors d'ouevre, snack or meal. Our recipe calls for purchased puff pastry and commercial hot pork sausage combined with ingredients found in every pantry.

1 pound roll hot pork breakfast sausage, or 1/2 pound sausage and 1/2 pound ground beef
1 medium onion, finely diced
1/2 medium red bell pepper, finely diced
2 cloves garlic, minced
1 small Louisiana yam, (or sweet potato) peeled and coarsely grated
1 teaspoon fresh basil, chopped
1/4 teaspoon Cayenne
1/4 teaspoon cracked black pepper
1/4 teaspoon white pepper
2 teaspoons Worcestershire sauce
3 sheets puff pastry, 9 x 9 inches, from the grocery freezer section
1 egg beaten with 1 tablespoon of water for egg wash

Place a large skillet over medium heat and sauté the meat, crumbling it into small pieces as it cooks. Remove from pan and drain on paper towels. Drain all but 1 tablespoon of fat from the pan and add the onions, bell pepper and garlic and cook until soft. Add the grated yam and cook 10 to 15 minutes. Add the basil, pepper and Worcestershire and stir well. Remove from heat. Taste and adjust seasoning.

Preheat oven to 375°.

On a lightly floured surface, roll out the puff pastry to about 1/8-inch thickness. Using a 4-inch plate as a guide, trace and cut out 4 circles of pastry from each of the 3 sheets. Transfer the 12 pastry circles to 2 parchment-lined baking sheets. Place a heaping tablespoon of filling on one side of each dough circle. Brush egg wash around the outer edge. Fold the dough over to enclose the filling and press with fingers or the tines of a fork to seal securely. Brush each pie lightly with egg wash.

Bake in the oven for 30-35 minutes or until golden brown.

Lagniappe: For the kids (big or small) gather the scraps of puff pastry and form a ball, then roll out into a rectangle, brush with egg wash, sprinkle with cinnamon sugar and cut into 1-inch strips. Twist the strips into spirals, place on a baking sheet, and bake at 350° for 20 minutes.

Crawfish Pies

YIELD: 12 PIES

NOTE: Shrimp may be substituted for crawfish

2 tablespoons unsalted butter
1 stalk celery, finely chopped
4 green onions, white and green parts only, thinly sliced
4 cloves garlic, very finely chopped
1 teaspoon grated lemon zest
1 teaspoon Tabasco Sauce
1/2 cup white wine or water
1 teaspoon salt-free Cajun Seasoning
1 pound fresh, peeled crawfish tails
4 ounces cream cheese, cut into 8 small chunks
3 sheets homemade or thawed frozen puffed pastry, at least 9 x 9-inches square
Egg Wash: 1 egg and 1 tablespoon cold water, beaten with a fork

Place a skillet over medium heat and add the butter. When it is hot, add the celery, green onions and garlic and cook for about 4 minutes, until softened. Stir in the lemon zest, Tabasco, wine and Cajun Seasoning. Bring to a simmer and add the crawfish tails. Stir for about 2 minutes, until warmed through, then stir in the cream cheese and continue stirring until the cheese has melted. Remove the pan from the heat and let cool to room temperature.

Preheat the oven to 375°

On a lightly floured surface, roll out the puff pastry to about 1/8-inch thickness. Using a 4-inch plate as a guide, trace and cut out 4 circles of pastry from each of the 3 sheets. Transfer the 12 pastry circles to 2 parchment-lined baking sheets. Place a heaping tablespoon of filling on one side of each dough circle. Brush egg wash around the outer edge. Fold the dough over to enclose the filling and press with fingers or the tines of a fork to seal securely. Brush each pie lightly with egg wash.

Bake for 30 minutes, or until puffed and golden brown. Let stand for 5 minutes, then serve on a doily-lined platter, if desired.

Seafood Gumbo

SERVES 6 TO 8

Gumbo is always served over rice. In fact, with a salad and hot French bread, there's no more satisfying meal. You may substitute any protein in any pleasing combination desired. For a seafood gumbo, use fish or shellfish stock; for chicken or sausage gumbo use chicken stock. To clean crabs, pull off the legs and the gills and discard, then cut the bodies into quarters.

2 quarts Shrimp or fish stock (see page 204)
4 tomatoes, diced (or use a 16-oz can, drained)
4 tablespoons bacon drippings or olive oil
4 tablespoons all-purpose flour
1-1/2 cups finely chopped celery
2 cups finely chopped onion (about 1 large onion)
2 cups finely chopped stemmed and seeded green pepper (about 3 peppers)
2 small cloves garlic, very finely chopped
1-1/2 teaspoons dried thyme
2 bay leaves
5 crabs, cleaned and quartered (see Note)
10 ounce package frozen cut-up okra
1/2 cup finely chopped green onion
1/2 cup finely chopped parsley
1 teaspoon freshly ground black pepper, or to taste
1/2 teaspoon Cayenne pepper
2 pounds shrimp (40/50 count), shells removed
Cooked rice, for serving

In a large soup pot, combine the shrimp stock and diced tomatoes. Bring to a simmer over medium heat.

In a heavy saucepan, make the Roux: Melt the bacon drippings or olive oil over medium heat. Add the flour and cook, stirring frequently, until the Roux reaches the color of chocolate. Be careful not to let it scorch. (This will take anywhere from 30 to 45 minutes.) Add the celery, onions and green peppers and cook for about 10 minutes, stirring frequently, until softened. Stir in the garlic and add the thyme and bay leaf. Carefully add the Roux mixture to the soup pot—it tends to spit and pop when it hits the liquid—and cook for 10 minutes over medium heat, stirring occasionally.

Stir in the crab pieces, okra, green onion and parsley and bring to a boil. Skim off any impurities if necessary, then reduce the heat to a simmer. Cover the pot.

After 45 minutes, stir in the pepper, Cayenne and shrimp. Taste before adding salt (the salt in the stock and tomatoes may be sufficient).

Cook gently, covered, for about 20 minutes more. Taste and adjust seasonings if necessary before serving over fluffy boiled rice.

Sausage and Turkey Gumbo

YIELD: 2 GALLONS

Gumbo is one of those exemplary dishes that can be made in a number of ways and varies from cook to cook. The emphasis is on the main ingredients: meats, poultry, seafood or almost any combination of them all. Roux and the trinity of seasonings create a smoky, dense taste, rich in texture and bites of flavor. Messing around with mama's recipe will get almost anyone in trouble.

Families get together for holidays and cook up a continuous two or three-day food fest beginning with visits to the farmer's markets and grocery stores and ending with soups and turkey gumbo from the leftovers.

1 whole turkey carcass, cut in half
2 cups corn oil
3 cups all-purpose flour
2 large onions, chopped
3 green bell peppers, stemmed, seeded and chopped
4 stalks celery, chopped
2 cans of your favorite local beer or an equal amount of stock or water
3 tablespoons Worcestershire sauce
1/4 cup Tabasco or Crystal hot sauce
1 pound andouille or Hillshire Farms smoked sausage, thinly sliced and then cut crosswise into half-moons
2 tablespoons very finely chopped garlic
1-1/2 gallons chicken broth (homemade or canned; this should include the liquid in which the turkey carcass was cooked)
1 tablespoon dried basil
1 tablespoon dried oregano
1 tablespoon dried thyme
1/4 teaspoon Cayenne pepper
Cooked rice, for serving

In a large pot, simmer the turkey carcass halves in water to cover until the remaining meat falls off the bones. Drain, reserving the cooking water. Remove the meat from the bones, discard the bones. Shred the meat (this should yield 2 to 3 cups of turkey, but any poultry meat may be substituted).

In a heavy saucepan, make the Roux (see page 216). Melt the oil over medium heat. Add the flour and cook, stirring frequently, until the Roux reaches the color of milk chocolate. Be careful not to let it scorch. (This will take anywhere from 25 to 30 minutes.)

Add the chopped onions, peppers and celery to the Roux (this will stop the cooking process). Cook until the vegetables are tender, stirring occasionally. As they cook, sugar will be released and the Roux will darken even more as the liquid evaporates. Stir in the beer (or water), Worcestershire and hot sauce.

In a large Dutch oven or the original soup pot, sauté the sausage and garlic in one tablespoon of oil until the garlic is transparent. Carefully add the Roux mixture to the pot, stirring (it will spit and sputter). Add the poultry broth and stir in the herbs and Cayenne pepper. Simmer covered for one hour, then add the shredded turkey and cook for 20 minutes more. Taste for seasoning and add more salt and pepper as desired

Serve in bowls over fluffy cooked rice.

Creole Stuffed Crab

SERVES 4

This mixture also makes a wonderful stuffing for shrimp or mushrooms.

1 tablespoon Arnaud's Creole mustard
1 large egg
1/2 cup mayonnaise
1 tablespoon fresh lemon juice
1/2 small red onion, finely chopped
1 green pepper, seeded, de-ribbed and finely chopped (or use 1/3 red, 1/3 yellow and
    1/3 green peppers)
1 teaspoon finely chopped fresh cilantro
1 teaspoon Kosher or sea salt
1/2 teaspoon freshly ground black pepper
1 cup fine, dry breadcrumbs, plus extra for the baking sheet
1 pound lump crabmeat, picked over for bits of shell and cartilage
1/2 cup olive oil or clarified butter
4 sprigs of fresh basil, for garnish
8 crab shell backs or 6 ounce ramekins

If planning to cook right away, preheat oven to 375°.

In a large bowl, whisk together the mustard, egg, mayonnaise and lemon juice until smooth. Stir in the onions, green pepper, cilantro, salt and pepper. Gently but thoroughly fold in 2/3 cup of the breadcrumbs and the crabmeat. Place the remaining breadcrumbs in a shallow bowl. With clean hands, portion out and form the crabmeat mixture into 8 round cakes, about 2 inches tall and 4 inches wide. (If you plan to cook the crab later, at this point you may cover them with plastic wrap—piercing the wrap in several places to prevent the mixture from getting soggy—and refrigerate up to overnight.

Line a large baking sheet with parchment paper and dust lightly with breadcrumbs.

Place a large sauté pan over medium high heat and add the olive oil or clarified butter. Sauté the crab mixture in batches, for about 1 minute on each side, until golden brown. As they are finished, gently transfer to fill the crab shells or ramekins. When all the mixture has been browned and stuffed into the shells, dredge each crab shell top in the reserved breadcrumbs, just to lightly coat, and place on the baking sheet. Finish cooking in the hot oven for 5 minutes.

Garnish with a sprig of basil and serve.

Shrimp Creole

SERVES 6

Shrimp Creole is a beloved example of New Orleans home cooking.

4 tablespoons extra-virgin olive oil
3 pounds cooked and shelled medium shrimp
3 cups Creole Sauce (recipe at right)
Kosher or sea salt and freshly ground black pepper
4-1/2 cups hot, cooked white rice, for serving
1/2 cup finely chopped flat-leaf parsley, for garnish

Warm 6 shallow soup bowls in a low oven.

Place a large skillet over high heat and add the olive oil. When it is hot, add the shrimp and stir for 1 minute, just to heat through. Add the Creole Sauce and bring to a boil. Reduce the heat to low and simmer gently for 3 minutes. Taste, and adjust seasoning with salt and pepper. Place 3/4 cup of rice in each warmed bowl and top with a generous spoonful of shrimp and sauce. Scatter generously with chopped parsley and serve.

Creole Sauce

YIELD: ABOUT 4 CUPS

Creole Sauce is a standard ingredient, used in many New Orleanian dishes. It will keep in the refrigerator for up to 3 days and freezes well.

2 tablespoons olive oil
1 small white onion, chopped
1/2 green pepper stemmed, seeded, de-ribbed and chopped
6 stalks celery, chopped
1/2 cup finely chopped flat-leaf parsley
1 clove garlic, very finely chopped
2 cups Veal Stock (see page 205)
1-1/4 teaspoons granulated chicken bouillon
1 Bouquet Garni (see page 217)
1 plum tomato, peeled, seeded and diced (or 1/2 cup canned, diced tomato)
1-1/2 cups tomato purée
Kosher or sea salt and freshly ground black pepper
Tabasco Sauce
Cayenne pepper

Place a large saucepan over high heat and add the olive oil. When it is hot, add the onion, green pepper, celery and parsley. Cook, stirring constantly, for two minutes. Add the garlic and cook for 30 seconds. Stir in the veal stock and chicken bouillon and add the bouquet garni, diced tomato and tomato purée. Bring to a boil, then reduce the heat to low and simmer the sauce, partially covered, for about 10 minutes, until nicely thickened. Season to taste with salt, black pepper, Tabasco Sauce and Cayenne. Use immediately, or cool to room temperature and refrigerate for up to 3 days, or freeze for up to one month.

Creole Jambalaya

Serves 6 to 8

Jambalaya is a Creole dish that appears often at casual parties and large get-togethers. It is about as versatile as your pantry allows: you can start with all fresh ingredients or use leftovers. We make seafood jambalaya, or sometimes we mix several ingredients, such as shrimp and chicken or sausage, or ham and chicken. Try this version to start, then let your taste buds or the contents of your refrigerator be your guide.

2 tablespoons vegetable oil
1/2 pound seasoned, smoked sausage such as andouille, diced
2 cloves garlic, very finely chopped
1/2 cup chopped green onion
1 cup chopped green pepper
1/4 cup chopped fresh parsley
1-1/2 cups chopped, canned tomatoes with liquid
1 bay leaf
1 teaspoon crushed thyme
1/8 teaspoon Cayenne pepper
1/2 teaspoon Kosher or sea salt
1-1/2 cups fish stock (see page 204, water may be substituted but is not ideal)
1 cup long grain rice
2 pounds jumbo shrimp, peeled and deveined

In a Dutch oven or a large heavy pan with a tight-fitting lid, warm the oil over medium-low heat and sauté the sausage for about 3 minutes, until warmed through.

Stir in the garlic, green onion and green pepper. Cook until tender, stirring occasionally, about 7 minutes.

Add the parsley, tomatoes, seasonings, broth and rice. Stir the mixture thoroughly, then add the shrimp.

Bring to a boil, reduce the heat to very low and cover the pan tightly.

Cook without stirring (or transfer to a 350° oven) for 25 to 30 minutes or until the rice is fluffy. Remove bay leaf, fluff and serve.

Boiled Seafood

YIELD: SERVES A CROWD

Arnaud's favorite staff get-together is a seafood boil at a member's home. Occasionally crawfish, crabs and shrimp are in season at the same time so we celebrate. When only one or two specialties are in season it is still a good enough reason to celebrate.

Seafood is usually boiled outside. A large 10-15 gallon pot allows seafood plenty of room to tumble through the seasoned water. A freestanding burner that uses bottled propane is available at hardware and home-supply stores.

For seasoning the feast some cooks swear by liquid crab boil. Others only use the traditional dry mix in bags. We each add our own special ingredients to the mix. The most important is personal preference.

Small new potatoes, corn on the cob, whole heads of garlic, lemons, whole onions, links of hot sausage and even pork tenders may also go into the boil with the seafood.

CRABS: ALLOW 6 PER PERSON
CRAWFISH: ALLOW 5 POUNDS PER PERSON
SHRIMP: ALLOW 1 OR 2 POUNDS PER PERSON
Crawfish, shrimp and/or crabs for the crowd
2 pounds salt
6 bags crab boil (or equivalent in liquid)
6 to 10 whole garlic heads
6 lemons, halved
2 bunches celery with leaves
10 bay leaves
2 ounces black peppercorns
12 ears corn, shucked and all silk removed, cut in half or thirds
5 pounds small whole red potatoes with skin on, rinsed
3 pounds small to medium size onions with outside skin removed and cut in half

Fill the pot with water to the halfway mark. Add salt, seasonings, vegetables and any other ingredients. Bring to a rolling boil for 15 minutes. Add the seafood and return to a boil. Turn off heat, cover and allow to stand for 10 minutes. Drain.

Cover the table with several layers of newspaper as an al fresco table-cloth which also doubles as the serving platter and plates.

NOTE

Crabs and crawfish must be live when they are added to the boiling water. Before boiling, purge crabs or crawfish in a large tub of water by adding a half box of salt. The salt makes them expel any mud or impurities. Rest in the salted water for 10 minutes. Change the water by flushing the tub with running water from a garden hose until clear.

Po-Boys

Po-boys are a staple of the local lunch—on the go or in a corner grocery or café. "To go" means po-boys are wrapped in white butcher paper and handed across the counter to be eaten at will. A sit-down café will serve them on a plate, usually with a side of fries.

A baguette of French bread is split and lightly toasted, then dressed. In New Orleans a dressed po-boy means all the fixings—a slathering of mayonnaise, Creole mustard and/or ketchup, then crisp lettuce and sliced tomatoes. Once the bed has been properly prepared, a heaping layer of fried seafood such as oysters, shrimp or catfish is added. The French bread may also be scooped out to create a more generous carrier.

Roast beef po-boys require juicy slices and debris, (the meat bits

falling off the roast and scraped from the pan). A ladle of warm gravy further moistens the sandwich. Ham and cheese po-boys are not served with gravy but are dressed.

The combinations are endless. One version stuffs the po boy with French fries, adds mayonnaise and roast beef gravy.

Remoulade's menu provides an excellent sampling of po-boys, hamburgers and hot dogs along with the more traditional dishes.

Toast the Cocktail

New Orleans claims the honor of inventing the cocktail, and nothing here (nor anywhere else) has been the same since a local pharmacist mixed up the first concoction. The Count, having made his start as a liquor salesman, held a certain affinity for fine spirits. His daughter, Germaine, inherited his enthusiasm.

Arnaud's was one of the many restaurants providing a "Gentlemen Only" area, and here was the Grill Bar. Germaine scotched that notion soon after she assumed command, so today the *rendezvous* is the French 75, a smart champagne and cocktail haven for both sexes.

The drink, dubbed by American doughboys in WWI to honor a French 75mm artillery shell, was served before battle. As the war ended in 1918, Arnaud's opened and began serving this invigorating cocktail.

As New Orleans reveled in the Roaring Twenties this festive establishment was doing very well; then, the National Prohibition Act was passed. Many Orleanians didn't even nod in acknowledgement and continued on their rollicking way.

Throughout the 1920s liquor continued to be freely poured at Arnaud's, but rather carefully under the cover of locked private rooms, disappearing back bars and in china coffee cups rather than crystal stemware.

Through the Count was repeatedly fined for selling alcohol, his cavalier attitude remained intact. His mansion was even raided and a ransom in whiskey which had been stored there since before Prohibition was removed.

Nevertheless, he was finally tossed into jail and the restaurant briefly padlocked. Ultimately, he won over the jury with an impassioned explanation of his philosophy. He was acquitted as Prohibition ended and the Count turned his infamy into promotion for his restaurant.

The golden age of Arnaud's was underway.

Count Arnaud Cazenave, in front of his mansion, believed that wine and spirits are natural companions of good food and good living. The Volstead Act, making alcohol illegal, passed just a year after Arnaud's opened, creating nothing more than a minor annoyance.

His elaborate home at 544 Esplanade Avenue and Royal Street was later owned by Academy Award-winning actor Nicholas Cage.

French 75

Yield: 1 cocktail

New Orleans' heritage of living under the French flag has always sparked popularity of the French 75 cocktail. It is topped off with champagne and, contrary to widespread belief, is made with cognac, not gin. During WWI officers and soldiers going into battle were fortified, appropriately enough, with French champagne and cognac. The powerful drink's name stems from the 75mm howitzers that were placed along the Maginot Line.

The French 75 has always been served at Arnaud's, but it has returned to popularity with the resurgence of interest in cocktails. It would be difficult to imagine a happier combination than fine champagne and excellent cognac.

1-1/2 ounces cognac
1 teaspoon fresh lemon juice
1/4 teaspoon Simple Syrup (see below)
Champagne as needed, about 4 ounces
Twist of lemon

Place the cognac, lemon juice and Simple Syrup in a shaker filled with ice and shake only long enough to chill. Pour into a frosted champagne glass, top with champagne and add a lemon twist. Serve immediately.

Simple Syrup

Simple Syrup is used in many cocktail recipes and always in the very best fresh lemonade.

Granulated sugar
Water

In a small saucepan, combine granulated sugar and water in a ratio of two to one (i.e., 2 cups sugar to one cup of water) and bring to a gentle simmer.

Stir and simmer until the sugar is completely dissolved, about 3 minutes. Cool to room temperature before using and store any unused syrup in the refrigerator. It will keep almost indefinitely. Simple syrup is used in many cocktail recipes, and always in the very best fresh lemonade.

The First Cocktail

Creation of the first cocktail, the Sazerac, is credited to the enterprising Antoine Amedee Peychaud, the inventor of Peychaud's Bitters. It is no surprise that bitters became an ingredient in his 1870s cocktail recipe.

A native of France, he established Pharmacie Peychaud at 437 Rue Royale, serving his concoctions in a *coquetier* (egg cup, in French). Local adoption and alteration of the word *coquetier* resulted in the mispronunciation "cocktail."

Orleanians are famous for mangling words, as evidenced by the often confusing pronunciation of street names. Calliope is pronounced Cah-lie-o-pee or Cal-ee-oope. However pronounced, it is either a riverboat's musical signal or one of the uptown street named after the Greek Muses (there are nine of them). Everyone here knows what, or where, you mean when you mangle.

Down the block from Peychaud's pharmacy was The Sazerac House, a coffee bar named after the brand, which helped to spread the word and popularize the new drink.

Many permutations of Sazerac bars ensued. One survives and continues to operate at the old Roosevelt Hotel, now a Fairmont.

The original recipe contained Sazerac cognac, absinthe, sugar and Peychard bitters. Pernod replaced absinthe when it was banned in America in 1912.

Traditionally, a Sazerac was served neat. That habit can easily be attributed to the scarcity of ice and the means to keep it frozen in this Southern city.

While the Sazerac was the first, it was certainly not the last in an ever-evolving list of fancy mixed drinks and cocktails. Arnaud's recipe is one of the few specifying two brands of bitters.

Sazerac

1 COCKTAIL

The Sazerac was invented in New Orleans and was the country's first cocktail.

2 ounces rye whiskey
1 teaspoon Simple Syrup (see page 168)
3 dashes Peychaud's bitters, if available, otherwise, double the Angostura
3 dashes Angostura bitters
Splash of water
2 dashes of Herbsaint or Pernod liqueur
Twist of lemon

In a pitcher half filled with ice, combine all ingredients except the Herbsaint and lemon twist and stir well. Pour the Herbsaint into a chilled rocks glass and swirl to coat the interior of the glass, discarding any excess. Strain the mixture into the glass, add the lemon twist and serve immediately.

Ojen Frappé

YIELD: 1 COCKTAIL

Ojen is an anise liqueur from Spain with a subtler flavor than French Pernod. Instead of turning yellow when mixed with water like Pernod, Ojen turns pink.

2 ounces Ojen liqueur
1 tablespoon Simple Syrup (see page 168)
1 ounce club soda

Combine the ingredients in a highball glass and add plenty of crushed ice. Stir and serve.

Eye-Openers

These classic cocktails are associated with the first drink of the day; a salute to the sun; a fond farewell to the evening past; or an appetite stimulant. They are also enjoyed throughout the day and before, during or after any other meal.

Bloody Mary

6 TO **8** SERVINGS

New Orleans' morning-after habit makes the Bloody Mary one of the city's most popular beverages. Even those who choose not to use alcohol can be served a Virgin Mary, prepared in the same manner sans vodka. The actual Bloody Mary recipe served at Arnaud's is a secret, but the one below is very close, and allows individual creativity of adjusting the flavors and seasonings.

1 quart tomato juice
1 can beef bouillon
Juice of one lemon
1 teaspoon Worcestershire sauce
2 teaspoons hot sauce
1 tablespoon prepared horseradish
1/4 teaspoon celery salt
Freshly ground white pepper
1-1/2 cups vodka

Mix all ingredients in a 2-quart pitcher. Stir until well blended. Pour into ice-filled glasses and garnish as desired.

At casual brunches, place the Bloody Mary mixture—minus the vodka—in a pretty pitcher. Place the vodka next to the pitcher so guests may or may not add it to their drinks.

Marinated Green Bean Garnish

The Bloody Mary's characteristics lend themselves to any number of garnishes. Arnaud's signature marinated green beans add color and crunch to this spicy, savory drink. Other popular dressings include sliced celery sticks, peeled green onions or pickled okra.

2-1/2 pounds raw snap beans
1-1/2 cups white vinegar
3 ounce bag crab boil
1/2 teaspoon Kosher or salt
2 to 4 cloves garlic (adjust to taste)
2 to 3 bay leaves
1/4 to 1/2 teaspoon crushed red pepper

Mix all ingredients together in a large covered plastic container and marinate beans 10 to 14 days in the refrigerator. Makes a lot of pickled beans, excellent garnish for a Bloody Mary and any number of salads and cold dishes.

Will keep indefinitely in the refrigerator.

Brandy Milk Punch

YIELD: 1 COCKTAIL

1-1/2 ounces brandy (bourbon may also be substituted)
1-1/2 ounces Simple Syrup
6 drops vanilla extract
4 ounces half and half
Dash ground nutmeg

Shake all ingredients together with crushed ice in a cocktail shaker or other covered container. Strain liquid into a chilled water or iced tea glass and sprinkle with nutmeg.

Cosmopolitan

YIELD: 1 COCKTAIL

1 ounce Absolut Kurant Vodka
1 ounce Cointreau
1/4 ounce (splash) Rose's Lime Juice
1/4 ounce (splash) cranberry juice
Lime wedge, for garnish

Shake all ingredients together with crushed ice in a cocktail shaker or other covered container. Strain liquid into a chilled cocktail or martini glass. Garnish with lime wedge.

Mimosa

YIELD: 1 COCKTAIL

2-1/2 ounces champagne
4-1/2 ounces fresh orange juice
1/2 orange slice, for garnish
1 mint sprig, for garnish

Chill champagne and orange juice. Chill champagne goblet. Fill goblet 1/3 with chilled champagne. Top off with orange juice. Add orange and mint garnishes for color.

For exquisitely cold cocktails, keep liquor such as vodka, gin, rum and bourbon in the freezer along with cocktail glasses. Then place ingredients in a covered container with crushed ice and shake vigorously, for at least 30 seconds before straining into a cold glass.

Post Prandial

After-dinner beverages include cocktails, rare bourbon, cognac, port, single malt scotch and other fine liqueurs and are best savored with a fine cigar and conversation.

If a cocktail is preferred, these classics may be just the thing. An Old Fashioned, for example, is just as it is named. A traditional cocktail of the highest order, it is meant to be sipped. A Manhattan recalls sophisticated ladies, cigarette holders and mustached gentlemen with bow ties.

Old Fashioned

YIELD: 1 COCKTAIL

Dash of bitters
1 teaspoon granulated sugar
1 teaspoon water
Maraschino cherry
Orange wedge
2 ounces bourbon
Splash of soda

Put bitters, sugar and water in a glass and stir gently until sugar dissolves. Add splash of soda. Dress with cherry and orange wedge. Add enough ice cubes to fill the glass and pour in the bourbon.

Manhattan

YIELD: 1 COCKTAIL

1-1/2 ounces rye whiskey
1/2 ounces sweet vermouth
Dash of bitters
Maraschino cherries

Combine whiskey, sweet vermouth and bitters in a cocktail shaker with a scoop of crushed ice. Shake vigorously and strain into a chilled cocktail glass. Garnish with a cherry.

The French 75's handsome bronze bust of Sir Winston Churchill is a rare one, displaying a cigar-smoking prime minister. A futile search led the Casbarians to commission a beloved young New Orleans artist, the late Daniel Price, to sculpt Churchill's likeness with a cigar. The cigar used in the casting was one of Casbarian's stash, most assuredly a Churchill.

Ramos Gin Fizz

YIELD: 1 COCKTAIL

One of New Orleans' most revered and legendary drinks, this cocktail was invented by barman Henry Ramos in the 1880s. When Huey Long was governor of Louisiana, he often traveled to New York with a bartender from New Orleans, so he would never have to be without this drink.

1-1/2 ounces gin
2 ounces half and half
2 ounces whole milk
1 large egg white
1 tablespoon Simple Syrup (see page 168)
2 drops orange flower water (available in the baking section of supermarkets)
1/2 teaspoon fresh lemon juice

In a shaker half filled with ice, combine all the ingredients. Shake well for 30 seconds. Pour into a chilled champagne flute over several cubes of ice and serve immediately.

Richelieu Bar

In the weeks following Casbarian's acquisition of Arnaud's and the beginning of restoration, many locals were fascinated by the changes occurring to one of their favorite establishments. Casbarian knew that months of work were ahead, but he also wanted to accommodate the curiosity of his friends and patrons.

He came up with an ingenious idea: the Richelieu Bar was just about the only structure that did not require substantial work and it happened to have a street entrance. He had fancy skeleton keys produced, numbered, and mailed out to New Orleans *bon vivants*— along with an invitation to come take a look. He rehired Mr. Henry, the restaurant's long-time, former bartender and from then on the Richelieu was packed daily with New Orleanians, supervising the construction process from their perches at the bar. Mr. Henry retired in 1980.

During the early hours of each New Year's Day, Stephen K. Bellaire, C.P.A.—firmly planted in reality—conducts the restaurant's annual year-end inventory in the Richelieu Bar. Not given to flights of fancy or wild imaginings, one year he was alone and counting bottles. Bellaire swears that he felt a dramatic drop in temperature emanating from the end of the long bar. When he turned around, a half-full cocktail glass had appeared on the until-then-empty counter. With the hair on the back of his neck bristling, he departed immediately.

Other sightings have occurred in the Richelieu, notably those of tuxedo-clad gentlemen, who may be bon vivants of an earlier century or late departed waiters.

More than one waiter has been startled to see a gentleman dressed in a turn of the century tuxedo standing in the far left corner of the main dining room. He seems to appear when the restaurant is at its busiest and most exuberant and is smiling with a proprietary air.

One waiter saw an elegantly dressed woman, wearing a fetching hat, leave the ladies room. She strolled across the corridor and disappeared through the wall. Investigation revealed that the wall had been added in this decade. On the other side, at the spot where she vanished, is a staircase. The waiter, one not easily rattled, was so shaken that he took the rest of the evening off.

Sweet Conclusions

The Irma Room, named after the Count's wife, is a confection of seafoam green, ivory, and gold. At the far end of the room opposite the fireplace is a unique musician's balcony, perfect for a jazz trio or string quartet. The room accommodates 80 guests for dining. Following an elaborate meal, a flambé dessert is a spectacular conclusion.

Dessert can be the grand finale to an exquisite meal, or merely a sweet ending to a simple repast.

Perhaps because Arnaud's menu is so vast, providing surprises of taste and texture at every course, the desserts tend to be more straightforward than complex. But this is not to say they don't have their own special pizzazz.

Bread Pudding

SERVES 8 TO 10

There is an on-going argument in New Orleans regarding the suitability of adding raisins to bread pudding. This is exactly the delicious kind of quarrel Orleanians love to engage in so that they have a suitable excuse to prepare and taste different versions. While there are as many recipes for bread pudding as there are restaurants in New Orleans, this one is a particularly splendid example, a rich custard-laced square brought to the table draped in warm, buttery whiskey sauce. Arnaud's recipe uses raisins; if preferred they can be left out.

2 large egg yolks
5 whole large eggs
1/2 cup granulated sugar
2-1/2 cups whole milk, scalded
1/2 cup heavy cream, scalded
3-1/2 cups stale French bread chunks
6 to 8 slices French bread, 1-inch thick
1/2 cup raisins
1/4 cup dark rum
4 tablespoons clarified butter, divided (see page 206)
1 tablespoons cinnamon
1 tablespoon sugar and 1/4 teaspoon cinnamon, mixed

Preheat the oven to 350°. Butter a 2-quart casserole. In a small bowl, pour the rum over the raisins and set aside to plump. In the bowl of an electric mixer set at low speed, mix together yolks, eggs and sugar. Add the milk and cream and mix well. Mix in the vanilla.

Combine the bread chunks, 2 tablespoon of the butter, cinnamon and rum-raisins in a large mixing bowl. Pour a generous amount of the pudding mixture over the bread. Stir to mix all ingredients and pour into the buttered casserole. Smooth the surface with the back of a spoon.

Dip the bread slices in the remaining pudding mixture and place over the pudding, overlapping to cover to the edges of the dish. Pour any remaining pudding over all. Drizzle with the remaining clarified butter and sprinkle generously with cinnamon sugar.

Cut parchment paper to fit the top of the dish, butter lightly and place over the surface of the pudding. Cover the dish tightly with aluminum foil and set the casserole dish inside a pan filled with hot water to within 1/2 inch of the top of the baking dish. Bake for approximately 50 minutes, remove the foil and bake 10 minutes longer.

Whiskey Sauce

YIELD: ABOUT 2 CUPS

Whiskey Sauce will keep at room temperature for 3 to 4 days. For those who are not fans of bourbon, rum or cognac makes a fine substitute. If desired, the alcohol may be eliminated entirely and a small amount of a flavoring such as almond extract substituted.

3 large eggs
1 cup (8 ounces, 2 sticks) butter, melted and still warm
1/2 cup granulated sugar
1-1/2 teaspoons bourbon

Using a mixer, whip the eggs at high speed until they are thick and pale. Reduce the speed to low and slowly add the warm butter. Gradually add the sugar and mix until cool, then slowly add the whiskey, blending it in thoroughly.

Caramel Cup Custard

Simplicity and elegance are underscored in this deceptively modest dessert. It comes to table molded as the cup shape in which it is baked, then overturned on a saucer for presentation. The silky smoothness of the custard is a revelation. It has long been a standard at Arnaud's and would be impossible to remove from the menu.

1/2 cup granulated sugar, for the caramel
1 tablespoon water
3 large eggs
1/4 cup granulated sugar
2 cups whole milk, scalded
1/2 teaspoon best quality pure vanilla extract

Preheat oven to 275°.

In a small, heavy skillet over low heat, stir the 1/2 cup sugar and 1 tablespoon water until the sugar melts, is free of lumps and turns a light caramel color.

Divide the caramel among six 4 ounce custard cups and let stand until cooled.

Beat the eggs with the 1/4 cup sugar and add the scalded milk slowly, while stirring. Add the vanilla and strain carefully into the prepared cups, to avoid disturbing the caramel.

Place cups in a pan of hot water. The water should come almost to the top of the cups. Cover with foil. Bake slowly for 1-1/2 to 1-3/4 hours, or until a knife inserted in the center comes out clean.

Remove from the water and cool to room temperature. Chill until serving time.

To serve, run a knife around the edge of the custard and invert the cup onto a small plate.

Tarte Tatin

SERVES 6 TO 8

France is responsible for the classic and humble apple tart.

1 pound homemade flaky pastry or bought puff pastry dough
3/4 cup (6 ounces, 1 1/2 sticks) unsalted butter, cut into 1/2-inch chunks
2 cups granulated sugar
2 tablespoons water
1 tablespoon fresh lemon juice
6 pounds Golden Delicious, Granny Smith, or any hard cooking apple, peeled, halved
    lengthwise and cored

Remove the dough from the refrigerator and let stand for 10 minutes. On a lightly floured surface, roll out the dough into a circle 1/4 inch thick and about 14 inches in diameter if you will be using a 12-inch tart pan (use a solid tart pan, preferably copper or a heavy skillet, not a pan with a removable base). Transfer the circle to a tray or baking sheet and refrigerate, covered with plastic wrap, for at least 15 minutes and up to 1 day, until ready to use.

Place the tart pan over medium heat and add the butter. When it has melted, stir in the sugar, water and lemon juice. Remove from the heat.

Slice off a small piece of one of the narrow ends of each apple half, to create a stable base. Arrange the apples upright in concentric circles in the mold, with their bases standing in the butter and sugar mixture. They should fill the mold and be tightly packed together. If there are halves left over, set them aside for the moment.

Place the mold over medium heat and cook for 35 to 55 minutes, until a medium colored caramel is formed. In the first few minutes, the apples will shrink and any stragglers may be fitted into the pan. Regulate the heat so that the liquid simmers briskly and, as always where caramel is involved, do not leave the kitchen (and keep an eye out for children near the stove—caramel gets very, very hot). At first, the liquid will be pale and thin from the juices of the apples. Keep cooking so that the water evaporates and the sugar and apple juices caramelize and are absorbed by the apples. Use potholders to move the pan around on the burners so the heat is evenly distributed, otherwise any hot spots may turn into burned spots. And remember that caramel keeps cooking for a minute or two after it is removed

from the heat, so stop cooking just before your ideal brown color is achieved. The color of the caramel, when finished, should be light to medium cinnamon.

Preheat the oven to 350° and place a rack in the upper third of the oven. Place the chilled circle of dough on top of the apples. Turn the rim of overhanging pastry back on itself to form a rough crust, keeping the apples completely covered. Bake for 15 to 20 minutes, until the pastry is crisp and brown. Let the tart cool for 5 minutes in the pan. Place a heat-proof serving plate upside down over the pan and invert the two together to unmold the tart onto the plate. Give it a good downward shake to help all the apples come away. If any apple sticks to the bottom of the pan, remove it with a metal spatula and replace on the tart. Serve warm or cold.

Crème Brûlée

SERVES 6

Crème Brûlée was added to Casbarian's menu right away—a personal family recipe, it was passed down from Jane's aunt. It was one of the first appearances of Crème Brûlée in a restaurant. The dessert has now swept the country and can be tricked out by adding fruit and other flavorful ingredients. At Arnaud's, Crème Brûlée is served classically just as it was designed. The literal translation from the French is "burned cream."

6 large egg yolks
1/3 cup granulated sugar
2-1/2 cups heavy cream
1 tablespoons vanilla extract
3 tablespoons dark brown sugar

Preheat the oven to 250°. In a medium bowl with the mixer set at medium speed, beat the egg yolks and sugar together and set aside. In a saucepan over medium heat, bring the cream to a boil. Remove from heat immediately and add to the egg-sugar mixture, continuing to beat. Add the vanilla and continue to beat until the mixture is completely cool.

Pour the cooled mixture into six 4 ounce custard cups. Line the sides of a 3 inch high baking pan with parchment paper, then place the cups in the pan. Add hot water until it reaches halfway up the sides of the cups. (The paper stabilizes the water and prevents the cups from shaking.)

Bake for 50 minutes. Remove the cups from the pan, let cool to room temperature and refrigerate until chilled.

Sprinkle 1/2 tablespoon of the brown sugar over the top of each cup. Place the cups on a baking sheet and set under a hot broiler until the sugar melts, darkens and forms a crust. (This is the brûlée process.)

Refrigerate until ready to serve.

Chocolate Devastation

If Créme Anglaise (see page 195) is not in your cooking schedule, whipped cream is a lovely substitute. Pictured above, the Chocolate Devastation is served with whipped cream and a puddle of coulis—simply sweetened and puréed fruit such as raspberries or strawberries—a counterpoint of color and flavor.

SERVES 8

The name says it all.

Impossibly rich, dense chocolate paté is cut into slices no more than 1/2-inch thick. It is wonderful to enjoy when it is lolling about in a pool of whipped cream or Crème Anglaise. (See page 195.)

1 pound bittersweet chocolate, chopped
2 sticks (8 ounces, one cup) plus 3 tablespoons unsalted butter, chopped
6 large eggs

Place chocolate and butter in the top of a double boiler with hot water in the bottom pan. Melt over low heat, stirring occasionally. Pour into a large bowl and set aside. Wash the top pan for the next step.

Break the eggs into the top pan of the double boiler and whisk. Over low heat, with hot water in the bottom pan just below but not touching the base of the top pan, whisk the eggs constantly until they are warm. Don't let the eggs get too hot or they will scramble.

With the mixer at medium speed, whip the warm eggs until tripled in volume with firm peaks. Carefully fold the whipped eggs into the chocolate just until mixed, to prevent losing volume.

Fill a clean, dry 4- by 12-inch terrine about 3/4 full, wrap the top in plastic and refrigerate until set. (May be made in smaller loaf pans or terrines filled to 3-inch depth.)

Strawberries Arnaud

Serves 6

Louisiana-grown strawberries are sweet, plump and succulent. When they are in season it is a shame to order anything else. Strawberries Arnaud celebrates them in a simple and refreshing recipe designed to crown any meal.

1 cup ruby port
1 cup red burgundy-style wine
1/2 orange, sliced
1 lime, sliced
1 whole clove
1 cinnamon stick
1/2 cup granulated sugar
3 cups vanilla ice cream
3 cups sliced fresh strawberries
Lightly sweetened whipped cream, for garnish
Six whole, perfect strawberries with their stems, for garnish
Sprigs of fresh mint, for garnish

In a medium saucepan, combine the port and wine and place over medium-high heat. Bring to a boil, then add the orange and lime slices, the spices and sugar. Return to a boil, then remove from the heat and cool for at least 30 minutes. Strain the sauce, cover and refrigerate until serving (the sauce will keep for up to 2 weeks).

To serve, place one scoop of ice cream in each of 6 champagne glasses. Cover the ice cream with sliced strawberries and drizzle generously with the port sauce. Add a dollop of whipped cream, a whole strawberry, if desired, and a sprig of fresh mint for show and serve at once.

Creamy Pralines

YIELD: ABOUT 36 2-INCH CANDIES

Every native Orleanian has fond memories of watching the making of pecan pralines; all also affirm their recipe to be the definitive Orleans confection. Consequently, a myriad of recipes abound in various cook books sharing one common thread: they are conspicuously short on directions for successful technique. To ensure success, pre-measure and assemble all the ingredients before you begin melting the sugars. Be extremely careful of this boiling-hot mixture; if splashed, it will stick to the skin and continue burning. Keep children and dogs away from the kitchen and see the note below for Things That Can Go Wrong.

Softened butter or non-stick vegetable oil spray

2 cups ripe, shelled pecans

1/4 cup (2 ounces, 1/2 stick) unsalted butter

2 cups granulated sugar

2 cups packed light brown sugar

14 ounce can condensed milk

3/4 cup water

2 teaspoons vanilla (we prefer Mexican vanilla)

Preheat the oven to 350°. Spread several large sheets of waxed paper on a flat surface. Spread the papers evenly with softened butter, or spray with a non-stick vegetable spray.

Spread the pecans on a baking sheet and toast for 10 minutes, until slightly golden and aromatic (watch carefully and do not scorch!). Break into pebble-sized pieces if necessary.

Place a deep and heavy saucepan over medium heat. Add the butter and as soon as it has melted, stir in the granulated and brown sugars, the condensed milk and the water. Stir constantly for about 5 minutes, until all the sugar has dissolved and the mixture comes to a boil. Continue boiling and stirring for 15 to 20 minutes until the mixture reaches 240° on a candy thermometer, also known as the "softball" stage. Add the pecans.

As you approach the proper temperature, the candy gets thicker and the bottom of the pan can be seen as you stir. Drop a small test praline on the waxed paper. If it is very shiny and stays shiny, keep cooking and stirring. When the proper temperature is reached the pralines will suddenly become quite stiff, so work fast: Spoon out

rounds onto the waxed paper, spreading gently until flat and about 2 inches in diameter. Let cool. Store in a tightly covered container. They will keep several weeks. Uncovered, they will succumb to humidity and become sticky.

THINGS THAT CAN GO WRONG

If the praline mixture is undercooked, the result will be a shiny, sticky mess that resembles caramel sauce (which it is). Either use as a wonderful ice cream topping, or try scraping back into the pan, then reheat to the correct temperature. However, there is no guarantee it will reconstitute.

If it is overcooked, the praline mixture will result in grainy, sugary, crunchy pralines. The solution? Crumble and use as a topping for sweet potato casserole, or scatter over ice cream.

Lemon Soufflé

6 SERVINGS

3/4 cup sugar, divided
1 cup flour
2 whole eggs
4 egg yolks, whites reserved
8 egg whites
2 cups milk, divided
6 tablespoons butter
4 teaspoons lemon zest
4 teaspoons lemon extract

Preheat oven to 425° and prepare individual soufflé molds by wiping with butter and sprinkling with sugar.

Place the flour and half the sugar in a small mixing bowl. Add egg yolks and whole eggs and whisk until smooth.

In a saucepan, bring milk and the rest of the sugar just to boiling point. Remove from heat and add about 1/3 of the milk to the egg mixture, whisking until smooth.

Add the egg mixture back into the pan and return to heat, whisking constantly. When mixture thickens to the consistency of pudding, remove from heat and whisk in butter. Cool until tepid.

Beat egg whites to medium peak.

Place one cup of pastry cream into a large bowl and whisk in the lemon zest and lemon extract until smooth. Gently fold in beaten egg whites.

Place prepared soufflé dishes on a sheet pan and fill. Add about 1/4-inch water to the pan. Bake for 24 minutes. Remove. Dust with powdered sugar and serve immediately.

Note: The pastry cream recipe makes about three cups. It may be used to create other dessert dishes. Instead of beaten egg whites, fold in whipped cream and chill for a light, airy pudding; serve with your favorite dessert sauce, fruit purée or fresh fruit; serve over pound cake.

Palmiers (Palm Leaves)

MAKES ABOUT 10 PASTRIES

1 10-inch by 15-inch sheet puff pastry, homemade or purchased frozen and thawed
1 cup granulated sugar, divided
1/4 cup unsalted butter, for baking sheet
1/2 cup light corn syrup

Sprinkle 1/4 cup sugar on a clean work surface. Place the puff pastry on the sugar and dust the top with 1/4 cup sugar. Roll gently with a rolling pin to press the sugar into the dough. Roll the dough to 1/4-inch thickness, maintaining the rectangular shape.

On the long side of the dough, lightly mark the center from top to bottom and then mark each half in thirds. Starting at one outside edge, use the guidelines to fold the dough two times to the center line. Repeat from the opposite outside edge to meet at the center. There will be three layers on each side. Fold one set of three layers over and form a log of six layers, open along one side.

Cut the puff pastry log crosswise into 1/2-inch slices Place the slices on a buttered baking sheet and spread slightly on the open side. Sprinkle with 1/4 cup of the sugar. Let rest at room temperature for about 20 minutes.

Bake at 400° until the bottoms caramelize, approximately 5 minutes. Turn over and bake 3 to 4 more minutes, until golden brown.

Remove from the oven. Brush palmiers with corn syrup and sprinkle with the remaining 1/4 cup sugar.

Creative cooks have discovered the squeeze bottle for use in decorating plates. At left, pools of a raspberry coulis are outlined with a warmed chocolate sauce.

Any puréed and colorful ingredients can be placed in squeeze bottles and used to decorate the plate with dots, zig-zags, squiggles, names and anything else you can apply with a steady hand.

Olé Flambé!

During Mardi Gras flambeaux (torch) carriers light the way for evening Carnival parades, festively dancing along ahead of the floats and marchers. This may be one reason why Orleanians so enjoy the ceremony of dishes flamed at tableside. Flaming desserts are always an elegant exclamation point for a meal.

The process seems simple: liqueur is ignited, and much of the alcohol is burned off, leaving behind a warm essence of flavor. There are strict rules to be followed for safe flambé-cooking. Never add liquor to the flambé pan while it is over the flame. Always flame the liquor in a ladle, then pour the flaming contents into the pan.

We recommend that this magic be performed well away from draperies, low ceilings, intake air vents, overhanging decorations, and your guests' coiffures or clothing. Consider using a cocktail cart or separate table for staging the show.

A flambé pan and a side burner make excellent accessories for tableside flambé productions; they are available at most kitchen and gourmet shops. Otherwise, the same effect may be achieved with a chafing dish set over a flaming pot of sterno, or a heavy skillet or crêpe pan on the stove.

Arnaud's Café Brûlot

SERVES 4

As much a ceremony as a drink, Café Brûlot (say brew-low) has put the flaming touch on many New Orleans dinners. Legend has it that the famous buccaneer Jean Lafitte originated this spectacular after-dinner drink; in French, Brûlot translates as "burnt brandy." At Arnaud's, a special Brûlot ladle that strains out the spices is used to pour the drink into the traditional tall, narrow Brûlot cups.

Two-inch stick of cinnamon
6 whole cloves
3 tablespoons slivered or grated orange peel
1/4 cup slivered or grated lemon peel
3 sugar cubes
1/2 cup brandy
2 tablespoons Curaçao, Grand Marnier or Cointreau
3 cups hot, strong black coffee
1 long, fireplace match

In a copper Brûlot bowl or chafing dish, combine the cinnamon, cloves, citrus peel and sugar cubes. Place over medium heat and crush together, using the back of a large ladle. Add the brandy and Curaçao to the ladle, light with a long match, then pour the flaming liqueur into the pan. Stir thoroughly and, simmer, stirring to dissolve the sugar. As the flames begin to die out, gradually add the black coffee. Ladle into Brûlot or demitasse cups, leaving the spices and citrus peels behind and serve at once.

FLAMBÉ SHOWMANSHIP

As part of the never-ending show, Arnaud's waiters peel a long, continuous curl of orange peel and stud it with cloves every inch in a cross pattern. The curl is held the over the Brûlot bowl and flaming brandy is poured (from a ladle) down the spiral and into the bowl. Ambitious home cooks who would like to duplicate this visually stunning spectacle may prepare the orange skin in advance and set it aside until serving time. Using a sharp paring knife, take care to peel only the orange skin and membrane, avoiding the inner white pith. Spear the peel on a fork (preferably silver) and hold above the prepared mixture in the Brûlot bowl, then slowly ladle the flaming brandy onto the peel, so it drizzles down the spiral into the bowl.

Bananas Foster

SERVES 6

Flaming adds a touch of drama and excitement to this exquisite dessert. Do use the best ice cream available (substitute banana ice cream for vanilla, if desired).

5-1/2 teaspoons ground cinnamon
1 tablespoon granulated sugar
6 tablespoons (3 ounces, 3/4 stick) unsalted butter
3 cups light brown sugar
6 whole bananas, peeled, halved lengthwise and then cut into quarters
1/3 cup dark rum
1/4 cup banana liqueur
6 scoops vanilla ice cream, slightly softened
2 long, fireplace matches

In a small bowl, combine the cinnamon and sugar, mix thoroughly and set aside.

In a flambé pan or a chafing dish, combine the butter and brown sugar. Mash together, then place the pan over medium heat and stir with a wooden spoon until the sugar melts and the mixture caramelizes to a rich brown color.

Add the banana pieces to the pan, cut sides down and cook for about 1 minute. Place the rum in a large ladle and ignite with a long match. Drizzle the flaming rum into the pan.

Scatter the cinnamon-sugar mixture directly over the flame. As the flame dies out, pour the banana liqueur into the ladle and ignite with a long match. Drizzle the flaming banana liqueur into the pan and stir gently to combine all the ingredients. The flames will quickly die down.

Immediately place one scoop of ice cream in each of six saucer-style champagne glasses. Spoon over some of the banana mixture and plenty of the pan juices and serve immediately.

Baked Alaska

Occasionally, Arnaud's chefs will prepare Baked Alaska to celebrate a special event. The surprise: a central core of ice cream rests on a bed of sponge cake and is hidden under swirls of cooked meringue! The contrast of textures is only surpassed by the spectacle of this flaming, multi-temperature presentation. As one might imagine, this is an ambitious dish and requires some advance preparation.

The home cook can assemble a Baked Alaska almost entirely with purchased ingredients (except for the very simple meringue). Depending on the occasion, pipe decorative hearts, swans or names on the surface of the meringue, using a little of the meringue in a pastry bag fitted with a plain nozzle.

(Please read safety guidelines for flaming on page 191 before preparing this dish.)

1 quart ice cream (flavor of your choice)
One-layer, 9-inch round sponge cake

MERINGUE:
3 large egg whites, at room temperature
1/2 teaspoon fresh lemon juice
6 tablespoons granulated sugar
2 tablespoons brandy
Chocolate Sauce, for serving (optional, recipe follows)
Shaved or grated chocolate, sprinkles, fresh fruit and nuts, for garnish if desired
1 long, fireplace match

In 1867 the chef at New York's celebrated Delmonico's (for posterity, his name was Ranhofer) elevated this dessert to super-star status. The original dish (known variously as omelette *á la Norvégienne*, Norwegian omelette, omelette surprise, and *glace au four*) was renamed "Baked Alaska" to celebrate the purchase of the Alaskan Territory. Largely ignored and rarely celebrated, Baked Alaska Day falls on February 1 (a good reason to give the dish a try!).

The night before: soften the ice cream at room temperature until it is easily scoop-able. Choose a 1-quart metal mixing bowl that is 1 inch smaller in diameter than the sponge cake, and pack the ice cream firmly into the bowl, smoothing the top. Re-freeze overnight, until completely solid. Refrigerate the sponge cake.

About 45 minutes before you plan to serve the dessert, place the sponge cake on a large, heatproof platter. Loosen the ice cream from its metal bowl by plunging the bowl into a bath of hot water for five seconds. Quickly invert the bowl on top of the sponge cake until it releases. Return the platter to the freezer while you prepare the meringue.

Preheat the broiler and place the oven rack at the lowest level.

In a very clean, medium mixing bowl (chill the bowl for best results) beat the egg whites and lemon juice until they have almost reached the soft peak stage. Gradually add the sugar in a slow, steady stream while you continue to beat the whites until they reach the firm peak stage.

Remove the cake and ice cream from the freezer. Working quickly, use a rubber spatula to coat the dome of ice cream and the cake base completely with meringue, swirling to create a wavy surface.

Watching constantly (do not leave this arrangement unattended even for a moment), place the platter under the broiler for two to three minutes until the peaks of meringue turn a pale golden brown. If necessary, turn once or twice for even browning.

Proceed directly to the table, pour the brandy into a ladle and light it with a long match. Drizzle the flaming brandy all around the edge of the Baked Alaska and scoop individual portions into waiting bowls.

Decorate with shaved or grated chocolate, sprinkles, or fresh fruit, if desired.

If desired, serve with a gravy-boat of luscious Chocolate Sauce, on the side.

Chocolate Sauce

YIELD: 2 CUPS

1 cup heavy cream
1/2 pound semi-sweet chocolate, broken into small pieces
3 tablespoons light corn syrup

In a small saucepan, bring the cream to a boil. Remove from the heat and add the chocolate pieces and corn syrup. Stir until the chocolate is melted and the mixture is smooth.

Keep unused sauce tightly covered in the refrigerator for up to 4 days.

Traditional Baked Alaska features vanilla ice cream, but any flavor may be substituted. Arnaud's guests enjoy the surprising color of peppermint ice cream. Neapolitan ice cream makes for an interesting tri-colored presentation—trust your taste buds and imagination.

Crème Anglaise (Basic Vanilla Custard Sauce)

YIELD: ABOUT 4 CUPS.

2-1/2 cups whole milk
1 cup heavy cream
2 vanilla beans (or 2 teaspoons vanilla extract, see below*)
8 large egg yolks, at room temperature
3/4 cup granulated sugar

In a medium saucepan, combine the milk and cream. Working on a piece of waxed paper or aluminum foil, split the vanilla bean down the center with the tip of a paring knife and scrape out as many of the seeds as possible. Dump the seeds and two halves of the vanilla pod into the milk mixture. Over medium heat, bring up just to a boil, then immediately remove the pan from the heat (watch carefully to prevent a boil-over). Let the mixture stand for 30 minutes, so the flavor can infuse into the milk.

Place a medium, metal bowl into a larger bowl 3/4 filled with ice water. Place a fine mesh strainer inside the empty bowl. Set aside.

In another medium bowl beat the yolks and sugar together until the mixture is thick, fluffy, and pale yellow.

Remove the vanilla pod pieces from the milk mixture and return it just briefly to a boil.

Slowly whisk about 1/2 cup of the hot milk mixture to the egg mixture to temper the yolks. Then, while stirring constantly with a heat-resistant spatula, return the egg mixture back to the pan with the remaining milk/cream mixture.

Place the pan over medium-low heat and stir the mixture constantly until it reaches the consistency of heavy cream, or until a finger drawn along the back of the spoon leaves a trail. (If the mixture leaves a distinct path without the two sides running together, the cream is finished.)

Immediately strain the finished cream through the strainer into the iced bowl. (*If using vanilla extract, add it now.) Stir occasionally until cooled. Use immediately or store, tightly covered, for up to 2 days in the refrigerator.

Crêpes

YIELD: APPROXIMATELY 12 CRÊPES , DEPENDING ON THE SIZE OF THE PAN

Make the crêpes ahead of time, or use the convenient prepared ones that can be found in most grocery store freezer cases. If the pan is hot enough, the batter will make a hissing noise when poured into the skillet. In any event you will want to lower the heat to medium after cooking a few crêpes, or they will cook too quickly, toughen, and burn.

1 cup whole milk
1 large egg
1/4 teaspoon Kosher or sea salt
1 teaspoon vegetable oil
1 cup all-purpose flour, sifted
Vegetable oil, for frying

In a blender, combine the milk, egg, salt, oil and flour. Blend until smooth. The batter should be about the thickness of heavy cream; if you prefer thinner, more delicate crêpes, add a little more milk a few teaspoons at a time, until the batter is the consistency of half-and-half. Cover and let rest in the refrigerator for 30 minutes.

Wipe a small non-stick frying pan (5 to 7 inches in diameter) with a paper towel that has been moistened with vegetable oil. Place the pan over medium-high heat and, when it is hot, use a 1 ounce ladle to pour the batter for the first crêpe into the center of the pan. Immediately lift the pan from the heat and tilt and swirl it, to coat the base of the pan with a thin, even layer of batter. Return the pan to the heat.

After a minute or so, when the crêpe turns brown at the edges, gently loosen with a spatula, and flip it over. Cook the remaining side until any moisture disappears, only another minute or so. Transfer the finished crêpe to a lightly oiled plate, and make the remaining crêpes in the same way, wiping the pan with the oiled towel again as necessary.

Cover the stack of crêpes with a paper towel and cool to room temperature. If desired, cover with plastic wrap and refrigerate for up to 24 hours before using.

Popularized in America by Henri Charpentier, the French-born chef of John D. Rockefeller, the Crêpes Suzette were created either at the Café de Paris in Monte Carlo, or at La Maison Française in Rockefeller Center, circa 1896. One legend has it that Charpentier devised the dish in honor of a beautiful lady named Suzette who accompanied Edward, Prince of Wales II, to the Café de Paris. Yet another tale has the dish named by Charpentier to acknowledge a well-known courtesan.

Prince Edward denied ever having known a woman by the name of Suzette. Yet ten years after the creation of the dish, Edward ordered it at London's Savoy. He commented that "a single taste would reform a cannibal into a civilized gentleman."

Whether or not the stories are true, they make a fitting garnish when serving this decadent dessert. Coincidentally, Crêpes Suzette appeared on one of the Count's early menus.

Crêpes Suzette

YIELD: 12 CRÊPES (SERVES 6)

This is a personal favorite that Casbarian introduced onto the Arnaud's menu in 1979. To this day, Crêpes Suzette are his preferred dessert for festive occasions. (Please read safety guidelines for flaming on page 191 before preparing this dish.)

1/4 cup (2 ounces, 1/2 stick) unsalted butter
1 cup granulated sugar
1 teaspoon grated orange zest
1 teaspoon grated lemon zest
1/2 cup Grand Marnier
Juice of 1 orange
Juice of 1/2 lemon
12 crêpes (recipe at left)
1/4 cup brandy
6 paper-thin slices of orange, for garnish
6 paper-thin slices of lemon, for garnish
6 strawberries (optional), for garnish
6 sprigs of fresh mint (optional), for garnish
1 long, fireplace match

Make the crêpes, if you have not already done so and warm 4 plates in a low oven.

In a flambé pan or chafing dish, combine the butter and sugar. Place over medium heat and stir until the butter has melted and the sugar has dissolved. Add the lemon and the orange zest and carefully stir until slightly caramelized and golden (do not leave the pan unattended during this step). Add the Grand Marnier, orange and lemon juices and stir together.

Add the crêpes two at a time and simmer for about 30 seconds on each side, until warmed through. Fold the crêpes into quarters (the finished shape is triangular) and baste with the pan juices. Add, warm, and fold the remaining crêpes in the same way.

Pour the brandy into a ladle and ignite with a long match. Drizzle the flaming brandy over the crêpes and serve as soon as the flames die down, garnishing each plate with a slice each of orange and lemon. Add a strawberry and a sprig of mint, if desired.

Crêpes Arnaud

YIELD: 6 CRÊPES

Forgotten in the mists of recipe history, this one turned up in a search of old documents. Many of the old Arnaud's recipes that were tried and tested make use of ingredients and techniques no longer suited for a modern kitchen. We were delighted to find this recipe, which is just as delicious as on the day it was created.

6 crêpes (recipe at left)
1 large egg yolk
1 cup powdered sugar
2 cups whole milk
2 cups all-purpose flour
4 tablespoons melted butter
3 large whole eggs, beaten together
4 large egg whites
Curaçao (optional)

Preheat oven to 425°.

In a bowl, beat the egg yolk well and add the powdered sugar to make a paste slightly thicker than mayonnaise. In another bowl, stir the milk into the flour, add the melted butter and the whole eggs. Mix all together and beat again.

Put a generous spoonful of the mixture just off the center of each crêpe, folding over the sides and ends like a pocketbook. Place crêpes into the oven for four to five minutes, watching them carefully until they brown. They puff up like an omelette soufflé and literally melt in the mouth. To serve this Suzette-style, sprinkle them with a little powdered sugar, pour Curaçao over them, light, and let the alcohol burn a few minutes.

SAUCERS

SILVER COFFEE POTS

Coffee

New Orleans and coffee have been an item for centuries. During the Civil War, ground chicory root was added to coffee beans to stretch the precious commodity. Orleanians became used to the flavor of chicory and it continues to be a local standard. The potent coffee and chicory brew is often cut in half by the simultaneous addition of hot milk, poured into the cup at the same time as the coffee, using two separate pots to create café au lait.

Coffee also provided Arnaud's with another early publicity bonus. A national company filmed a coffee television commercial here, asking guests to guess what brand they were enjoying at Arnaud's. The restaurant received welcome exposure when it aired repeatedly across the country, soon after Casbarian had completed the first stages of his renovation.

The Basics -

Sauces, Stocks and Seasonings

Sauces, stocks and seasonings are the instruments with which cooks give their creations that old razzmatazz. Here, we believe that a meal unadorned, without seasonings and sauces, is flat. Remember, we even dress our sandwiches.

When Germaine visited Paris in 1949, dress-up nights at Maxim's captured her sense of drama. Upon her return, she redesigned a closed bar with its adjacent dining room to mimic the places she had frequented abroad. She named the new rooms the Richelieu and the Richelieu Bar.

A separate entrance with an impressive canopy introduced guests to formal night on Saturdays. Fancy dress was mandatory for ladies and dark suits, if not black tie, for gentlemen. Germaine had created another good reason to show off her wardrobe and her jewelry. Later, the Richelieu dining room fell into disrepair and was closed once again. The Richelieu Bar stayed open.

In the 1990s Casbarian renamed the long-shuttered room the Jazz Bistro, and opened its French doors to Bourbon and Bienville Streets. He gave the old room a new decor and rhythm, featuring a live jazz trio with dinner, a return to early Bourbon Street. Arnaud's full menu is also offered in the more relaxed Jazz Bistro, accompanied by lively music. The ambiance is different than than Arnaud's elegant main dining room, but a welcome addition for musically inclined guests.

The one story plastered brick building was a French book shop then a grocery and later a shoe and boot store. It was probably built during the Spanish domination of Louisiana (1762-1803) and is dated as the earliest Arnaud's building.

Arnaud's Sauce

Arnaud's Sauce, the Original Creole Remoulade, is the restaurant's most famous creation.

The term "remoulade" comes from the Picard dialect of France, where ramolas means, simply, horseradish. Actually, there are at least three versions of remoulade sauce likely to turn up in the culinary world—two of them on a regular basis. Beloved of the French, the mayonnaise-style sauce is classic. The Creoles set that recipe on its ear, turning the sauce into an attack on the sinuses with horseradish or Dijon mustard, and sometimes crumbled, hard-boiled eggs. Finally, a green remoulade, or remoulade verte, is either of the above with the addition of chopped parsley. For the record, the Creoles' sauce was born from the French sauce, and Count Arnaud's sauce can count them both as parents. The recipe for the remoulade-based Arnaud Sauce—a crucial element of the renowned Shrimp Arnaud—remains a secret.

Germaine thought the recipe so valuable that she excluded it when Arnaud's was sold to Casbarian. She demanded instead that her personal cook make, bottle, and sell the sauce to the restaurant.

Following her death, the executor of Germaine's estate (a trust officer of a local bank) found himself making the sauce at home. Soon afterward, Casbarian was able to secure the rights to make Arnaud's sauce in Arnaud's kitchen.

He then spent almost ten years working with a number of chefs, food technicians and other specialists to stabilize the recipe in quantity.

A perfectionist in matters of taste, Casbarian is satisfied that he succeeded. He applies the same refined judgment whether he's tasting food or vintage wines. His taste test for the remoulade sauce is that the heat should peak on the third bite.

Aficionados use the sauce with seafood of all kinds, for hors d'oeuvres, as a cocktail sauce for fried foods, a dip, a spread for sandwiches, drizzled over deviled eggs or whatever else inspires individual creativity.

For Arnaud's 85th anniversary in 2003, Casbarian completed the research and recipe for Arnaud's Creole Mustard, an essential ingredient in many of Arnaud's recipes.

They are both available at the restaurant, fine grocery stores and through Arnaud's website at www.arnauds.com.

Shrimp Arnaud has held first place on Arnaud's menu since the Count's time. It is considered the benchmark by which all other Creole remoulade sauces are measured. Shrimp Arnaud is made by marinating boiled shrimp in the sauce for 12 hours, securely covered, in the refrigerator.

The original remoulade instructions posted in Arnaud's kitchen.

Stock

Many important sauces begin with a good stock. If time precludes making it at home, a variety of stocks and demi-glace may be purchased frozen.

Court Bouillon

YIELD: ABOUT 4 QUARTS

This is the secret ingredient in many Creole dishes. It is a superb poaching liquid for fish, chicken or sweetbreads. It will keep in the refrigerator for up to a week. For your own cooking arsenal, freeze in 1 or 2 cup containers.

4 quarts water
1 carrot, sliced
3 stalks celery, sliced
1/2 small white onion, sliced
3 bay leaves
3 cloves
1/2 teaspoon whole black peppercorns
2 teaspoon Kosher or sea salt

Combine all ingredients in a pot and bring to a boil over high heat. Boil for about 30 minutes to allow the flavors to develop.

Strain. May be used immediately or cooled and stored to use later.

Chicken Stock

YIELD: ABOUT 3 QUARTS

2 pounds chicken bones
1 pound chicken legs
1 pound onions, coarsely chopped
1/4 pound carrots, coarsely chopped
1/2 tablespoon black peppercorns
4 bay leaves
1 head garlic cut in half
1/2 tablespoon dried thyme
1 gallon very cold water

Wash bones in several changes of water and chop coarsely. Chop the chicken legs coarsely. Place all ingredients in stock pot and bring to a boil. Adjust the heat so the liquid simmers gently and cook, partially covered, skimming occasionally as needed, for about three hours. Strain through a colander lined with cheesecloth or a fine sieve. Do not allow the stock to boil rapidly, or it will turn cloudy.

Fish or Seafood Stock

YIELD: 4 QUARTS

2 pounds fish trimmings, shrimp, lobster or crawfish shells, or gumbo (small) crabs rinsed and coarsely chopped
1/2 pound onions, coarsely chopped
1/2 pound leeks, coarsely chopped
1/2 pound celery, coarsely chopped
4 bay leaves
1 teaspoon whole dried thyme
1-1/2 teaspoon white peppercorns, whole
1 head garlic, cut in half
4 quarts very cold water

Place all ingredients in stockpot. Bring to a boil, reduce heat and simmer partially covered for 45 minutes. Skim carefully. Remove from heat and strain. Do not allow the stock to boil rapidly, or it will turn cloudy.

Note: In a pinch, clam juice may be substituted for fish stock.

Veal or Beef Stock

Yield: About 2-1/2 quarts

A nice venison stock can be made in the same way by substituting venison bones for the veal or beef bones.

2 pounds veal or beef bones
3 tablespoon Kosher salt
2-2/3 cups sliced onions
2 cups sliced carrots
1 cup sliced leeks
1-2/3 cups sliced celery
1 cup chopped flat leaf parsley
1 teaspoon dried thyme
2 bay leaves
1/2 head garlic, peeled
1/2 cup tomato purée
5 black peppercorns

Preheat the oven to 450°. Place the veal bones in a roasting pan, sprinkle with salt and roast until brown, at least 30 minutes.

Place the bones, 8 quarts water and all the other ingredients in a stockpot and bring to a boil over high heat.

Lower heat and simmer for 2 to 3 hours, skimming as needed. When stock is done, strain and return the broth to the pot. Cook over high heat until it is reduced to 1/3 of its volume.

Will keep in the refrigerator for up to 1 week or freeze in small quantities for convenience.

Veal Glacé de Viande

Bring 2 cups of veal stock (above) to a boil. Adjust the heat so it simmers briskly and reduce by about 3/4, to about 1/2 cup of very syrupy liquid. Will keep indefinitely in the freezer.

Saucier Gregory Rosary is responsible for preparing all of the stocks and sauces used in the kitchen.

Beurre Blanc

YIELD: 1 CUP

1/4 cup white wine
1 tablespoon shallots or white parts only of green onions, very finely chopped
1/4 cup heavy cream
1/4 pound (1 stick) unsalted butter, cut into 8 chunks
1 tablespoon lemon juice

Place wine, shallots and heavy cream in a small saucepan and cook over low heat until reduced by 1/4.

Remove pan from the heat and slowly add half (4 tablespoons) of the butter, whisking vigorously until the butter melts.

Return the pan to the stove over extremely low heat and add the remaining butter. Whisk constantly until the butter has emulsified into the sauce. Remove from the heat immediately and stir in the lemon juice. The sauce will be the consistency of a light Hollandaise.

Strain and hold until serving time. To prevent separation, keep warm in the top of a double-boiler over hot, but not simmering, water; or place near the faint heat of the pilot light.

Clarified Butter

Clarified or drawn butter is simply melted butter with the solids removed. Without these solids, clarified butter withstands high temperatures and maintains the delicate butter flavor.

Over low heat, warm unsalted butter until it melts.

Remove from heat and let stand for a few minutes to allow the milk solids to settle to the bottom.

Pour off the clarified butter into a container. Keep cool.

Lemon Butter

YIELD: 1 CUP

Nothing simpler or more sensational.

3/4 cup (6 ounces, 1-1/2 sticks) unsalted butter
Juice of one lemon
Kosher or sea salt and white pepper, preferably freshly ground
2 teaspoons chopped flat leaf parsley

Melt the butter over high heat and then add the lemon juice.

Season to taste with salt and white pepper and stir in the parsley.

Remove from heat and keep warm until needed.

Garlic Butter

YIELD: 1-1/2 CUPS

3/4 pound (12 ounces, 3 sticks) unsalted butter, softened
1 cup chopped flat-leaf parsley
1/4 cup Herbsaint liqueur (Pernod or Ojen may be substituted)
2 tablespoons finely chopped garlic
Kosher or sea salt and freshly ground pepper

Place the butter in a mixing bowl. Add the parsley, Herbsaint and garlic and mix with a fork or whisk.

Season to taste with salt and pepper.

Bordelaise Sauce

YIELD: ABOUT 2 CUPS

2 tablespoons unsalted butter
1/4 cup finely chopped shallots
1 cup red wine
1 Bouquet Garni (see page 217)
1 whole clove
1 black peppercorn
1/2 clove garlic
1 bay leaf
1 quart Veal Stock (see page 205)
1 tablespoon Glacé de Viande or Veal Demi-glace (see page 205)
Kosher or sea salt and freshly ground black pepper

Melt the butter in a small pan over medium heat. When the foam has subsided, add the shallots and sauté until translucent, about 5 minutes. Add the red wine, increase the heat to medium-high and bring to a boil. Add the bouquet garni, clove, peppercorn, garlic, bay leaf and veal stock. Bring up to a boil, then lower the heat to very low, and simmer until the volume is reduced by about half and the sauce coats the back of a spoon. Stir in the Glacé de Viande, season to taste with salt and pepper, and strain into a clean pan.

Note: If desired, cool the sauce to room temperature, then refrigerate in an airtight container. Warm in the top of a double boiler over gently simmering water, stirring.

Béarnaise Sauce

YIELD: ABOUT 1-1/2 CUPS

1/2 cup red wine vinegar
1/4 cup chopped fresh tarragon leaves
2 large shallots, finely chopped
1/2 teaspoon coarsely ground black pepper
5 large egg yolks
1-1/4 cups clarified butter (see page 206)
Kosher or sea salt and white pepper, preferably freshly ground

In a medium saucepan, combine the vinegar, tarragon, shallots and pepper. Place the pan over high heat, bring to a boil and cook until the liquid has almost completely evaporated, leaving a moist but not wet mixture. Remove from heat and set aside at room temperature until just barely warm.

Transfer the mixture to the top of a double boiler. Over gently simmering—but not boiling—water, add the egg yolks and whisk for a minute or two, until the mixture is pale yellow, slightly thickened and the base of the pan is visible as you whisk. Begin adding the clarified butter very slowly in a thin stream, continuing to whisk all the time. After about 1/3 of the butter has successfully been whisked into the emulsified sauce, you may add the butter a little bit more quickly. Season to taste with salt and white pepper.

Hollandaise Sauce

YIELD: 1-1/4 CUPS

Adding the lemon juice at the very end makes the freshest-tasting hollandaise.

3 tablespoons water
3 large egg yolks
Kosher or sea salt and freshly ground white pepper
Ice cubes, if needed
1/2 cup warm clarified butter (see page 206)
2 to 3 teaspoons fresh lemon juice, or as needed

In a small, heavy saucepan, combine the water, egg yolks and a pinch of salt. Whisk constantly over low heat until the mixture is foamy and thick enough to form a ribbon when the whisk is pulled from the mixture. It should be pale yellow with the consistency of a thin yogurt. (This is a crucial stage: once the mixture has thickened, if it continues to heat it will curdle.) Be ready to pull the pan off the heat and have an ice cube or two on hand. If the mixture goes beyond the thick and creamy stage and appears even a little bit granular, quickly drop an ice cube into the mixture and whisk it in. (This is the technique for saving the sauce.) When the mixture has reached the correct foamy consistency, cool the pan by tipping it to the side and carefully holding the base of the pan under cold running water for a few seconds. This will stop the sauce from cooking any further.

Off the heat, begin adding the warm (not hot) clarified butter drop by drop, whisking all the time. Add the butter very slowly for about 30 seconds, then add the rest of the butter in a very thin, steady stream, whisking until it is all incorporated. Whisk in 2 teaspoons of lemon juice, and taste. You should be able to taste the lemon, but it should not overpower the delicate sauce or taste sour. Add more lemon juice bit by bit, if necessary, to achieve the perfect balance. Adjust the seasoning with salt and add a pinch of white pepper. Serve immediately or hold in the top of a double-boiler over hot, but not boiling, water for up to 45 minutes.

Blender Hollandaise

YIELD: 3/4 CUP

If mastering the classic preparation is too much to contemplate, we offer this alternative that is foolproof and quite tasty.

1/2 cup (1 stick) unsalted butter
3 large egg yolks
2 tablespoons fresh lemon juice
1/4 teaspoon Kosher or sea salt
Dash of ground white pepper

Over medium heat in a small saucepan, heat the butter until it melts. Remove from the heat and immediately place the egg yolks, lemon juice, salt and pepper in the blender. Cover and blend at medium speed for about 5 seconds.

Reduce the blender speed to low and slowly add the hot melted butter through the opening in the cover. When all the butter has been incorporated, switch to high speed for 30 seconds. Serve immediately or hold in the top of a double-boiler over hot, but not boiling, water for up to 45 minutes.

Armoricaine Sauce

YIELD: 4 CUPS

This sauce is an Arnaud's favorite.

2 pounds raw crawfish, live if possible, in the shell
2 tablespoons olive oil
Scant 1/2 cup finely chopped shallots
2 tablespoons chopped white onion
2 tablespoons sliced carrot
2 tablespoons chopped celery
2 tablespoons chopped leek
2 tablespoons brandy
3 tablespoons white wine
1 tablespoon tomato purée
1 whole tomato
1-1/2 cloves garlic
2 cloves
1/8 teaspoon black peppercorns
1 cup fish stock (see page 204)
1 teaspoon prepared lobster base, optional (available at specialty food stores)
4 cups water
2 tablespoons Blond Roux (see page 216)
Kosher or sea salt and freshly ground black pepper
Cayenne pepper
1 long, fireplace match

Clean the crawfish by washing several times in clear water. In a large pot over high heat, bring the olive oil to the smoking point and add the crawfish. Cook until they are a deep red color. This will require about 10 minutes. Add the shallots, onion, carrot, celery and leek and stir 3 to 4 minutes, until softened and golden.

Add the brandy and carefully ignite with the match. Flame for 10 seconds, then extinguish by placing the lid on the pot.

As soon as the flames have died down, add the white wine, tomato purée. tomato, garlic, cloves and peppercorns. Stir together, then add the fish stock, lobster base and water. Bring to a boil. Reduce the heat, cover and simmer for 30 minutes.

Transfer to a blender, in batches if necessary, blending each batch for 2 minutes. Return to the pot and boil for 8 minutes then thicken with the Roux, stirring in 1 tablespoon at a time, until the sauce coats the back of a spoon. Strain through a sieve and season to taste with salt, pepper and Cayenne. Serve at once or, if desired, cover and refrigerate for up to 4 days.

Creole Sauce Robért

YIELD: 1 QUART

This is an essential ingredient in many Creole recipes. For convenience, make up this recipe and freeze in 1-cup quantities to have on hand.

2 tablespoons olive oil
1 cup finely chopped white onion
1/2 cup diced green pepper
1-1/2 cups chopped celery
1/2 cup chopped flat leaf parsley
1 clove garlic, chopped
2 cups Veal Stock (see page 205)
3/4 teaspoon chicken base or granulated chicken bouillon
1 Bouquet Garni (see page 217)
1/2 cup diced tomatoes
1-1/2 cups tomato purée
Kosher or sea salt and freshly ground black pepper
Cayenne pepper
Tabasco Sauce

Place a 2-quart saucepan over high heat. Add the olive oil and when it is hot, add the onion, green pepper, celery and parsley. Stir for 2 minutes, then add the garlic, veal stock, chicken base or bouillon, bouquet garni, diced tomatoes and tomato purée and bring to a boil.

Reduce the heat and simmer, stirring occasionally, for 10 minutes. Stir in salt, black pepper, Cayenne and Tabasco Sauce to taste. Serve immediately or, if desired, cool, cover and refrigerate for up to 4 days, or freeze in 1-cup quantities.

White Wine Sauce

YIELD: 2 CUPS

For most recipes, use chicken stock. For seafood dishes, fish stock is a better choice.

2 teaspoons unsalted butter
1 tablespoon chopped shallot
1 bay leaf
1 teaspoon whole peppercorns
3/4 cup white wine
1-1/2 cups chicken or fish stock (see page 204)
1-1/2 cups heavy cream
1 tablespoon cornstarch
2 tablespoons cold water

In a saucepan over medium heat, melt the butter and sauté the shallots until transparent, about 5 minutes. Add the bay leaf and peppercorns and sauté for 1 minute. Stir in the white wine, stock and cream. Increase the heat to moderate and simmer the sauce, stirring frequently, until reduced by about half. Make a slurry by dissolving the cornstarch in the cold water and add it slowly to the sauce, stirring all the time. Return to a simmer and stir for 3 minutes to allow the cornstarch to thicken the sauce and lose its raw taste.

Strain through a sieve to remove peppercorns and bay leaf and use immediately or, if desired, cool, cover and refrigerate for up to 3 days.

Mushrooms Duxelles

1/2 cup (4 ounces) clarified butter (see page 206)
1 medium onion, finely chopped
1/2 pound white or cremini mushrooms, brushed clean and finely chopped
2 cups heavy cream
1-1/2 teaspoon Kosher or sea salt
1-1/2 teaspoon white pepper, preferably freshly ground

Place a large sauté pan over medium heat and add the clarified butter. When it is hot, add the onions and cook until transparent, stirring frequently, about 7 minutes. Add the mushrooms and cook, stirring constantly until almost dry, 7 to 8 minutes. Add cream and bring to a simmer. Reduce over medium heat until the texture is creamy and thick, stirring occasionally, about 5 minutes. Add the salt and pepper and taste for seasoning. Use as directed in the recipe.

Béchamel Sauce

YIELD: ABOUT 2-1/2 CUPS

1/3 cup unsalted butter
1/3 cup all-purpose flour
2 cups whole milk
1/2 cup sliced white onion
1 Bouquet Garni (see page 217)
1 clove
1 bay leaf
1/2 cup white Roux, (see page 216)
Kosher or sea salt and white pepper, preferably freshly ground

Make a white roux: Melt 1/3 cup of butter in a saucepan over low heat. Stir in 1/3 cup of flour a teaspoon at a time to form a paste. When the paste begins to foam gently, stir for a minute or two without browning, to cook off the raw taste of the flour. Remove from the heat.

In a saucepan over medium-high heat, combine the milk, onion, bouquet garni, clove and bay leaf and bring to a boil. Reduce the heat so the milk is simmering and gradually add the Roux, whisking in one tablespoon at a time then simmering for a minute or two, until it reaches a consistency that will coat the back of a spoon. Whisk in salt and white pepper to taste. Use immediately.

Jelly and Relish

Savory or sweet jellies, pickles and relishes create a jeweled complement to most meats, fish and poultry dishes.

Professional kitchens know that a few jars and bottles of herbed vinegar, oils and preserves give the chef a special way to add zing to their recipes and presentations.

Peppers and herbs are so easy to grow here that they are seen in window boxes and gardens all over New Orleans. In lieu of gardening, there's a seasonal harvest waiting at most groceries and farmer's markets.

Look for produce of contrasting or complimentary colors for visual appeal.

Mango-Ginger Chutney

YIELD: ABOUT 4 CUPS

2 tablespoons olive oil
1 medium red onion, coarsely chopped
1 small clove garlic, very finely chopped
1 tablespoon grated or finely chopped fresh ginger, with its juice
2 mangoes, peeled, pitted and coarsely chopped
1 tablespoon granulated sugar
1/4 cup white wine vinegar
1 green onion, thinly sliced
2 tablespoons finely chopped cilantro

Place a skillet over medium heat and add the olive oil. Sauté the red onion, garlic and ginger for about two minutes, stirring. Add the mango and lower the heat to medium-low. Partially cover the pan and stew the mixture for about 20 minutes, until the mango has broken down slightly. Add the sugar and cook for 5 minutes more. Remove from the heat and stir in the vinegar, green onion and cilantro. Cool to room temperature, then refrigerate for at least 4 hours so the flavors will marry. Will keep for up to a week.

Sweet and Spicy Corn Relish

YIELD: MAKES ABOUT 7 HALF PINT JARS

Delicious with hot French bread and butter or served with ham, pork, poultry or lamb dishes

10 large or 12 medium ears of fresh corn
2 large Vidalia or other sweet onions, peeled and finely chopped
1-1/3 cups cider vinegar
1 cup granulated sugar
1/3 cup green bell pepper, seeded and finely chopped
1/3 cup yellow bell pepper, seeded and finely chopped
1/3 cup red bell pepper, seeded and finely chopped
2 teaspoons salt
1-1/4 teaspoon dry mustard
1/2 teaspoon Cayenne pepper
1/2 teaspoon Tabasco Sauce or Crystal hot sauce
1/2 teaspoon turmeric

Clean the corn, removing husks and all silk. With a sharp knife, scrape the kernels from the cobs into a large pot.

Add the remaining ingredients and bring to a boil. Lower the heat and simmer for 30 minutes.

Pour into hot, sterilized preserving jars, cover and seal.

Hot Pepper Jelly

YIELD: 8 HALF PINTS.

The glorious displays of vegetable, fruit and pepper jellies at the Green Market held Saturday mornings on Magazine Street, rain or shine, are an inspiration and a delightful accent.

To decorate the jars, press out interesting shapes from the colorful ingredients using tiny hors d'oeuvres cutters or cut freehand. The jelly and bits of fruits or vegetables provide a colorful confetti.

Used as an accompaniment to meats and other main courses, jellies are also used to make a party hors d'oeuvres. Mound two tablespoons of colorful pepper jelly on a block of cream cheese and serve with crackers or French bread crustini.

6 green, red and yellow bell peppers (2 of each for color)
12 fresh jalapeño peppers
2 cups water
5-1/2 cups granulated sugar
1-1/2 cup apple cider
1 (6 ounce) bottle Certo® or comparable home preservative product
1 pair thin latex gloves per person

Roast the bell and jalapeño peppers on a fork over the burner flame or under a hot broiler, turning constantly until the skin is blackened. (Charring releases the flavors.) Wearing gloves, pull apart the cooled peppers by first removing the stem end. Most of the seeds will slide out of the pepper. Peel off the blackened skin. Cut the peppers in half and scrape out the remaining seeds. Chop the peppers coarsely and purée to a smooth paste in a food processor. Transfer to a measuring cup and add enough water to make two cups of pepper purée. In a non-reactive pot, combine the purée, sugar and apple cider. Bring to a rapid boil, stirring to dissolve the sugar. Reduce the mixture for 10 to 12 minutes, or by about one third. Remove from heat and add Certo®. Boil for 1 more minute. Skim off foam.

Pour into hot sterilized half pint-size canning jars, leaving a one-fourth inch space at the top of each jar. Wipe the jar rims with a clean, damp cloth, fit them with hot lids, and tightly screw on the metal rings. Place in a bath of boiling water for 10 minutes (the water should cover the jars by about one inch), cool on a wire rack. Seal and store in a cool, dark place.

Roux

Roux is a mystical mixture of flour and fat that is cooked before adding to liquid. Depending on the recipe, the fat may be butter, clarified butter, bacon fat, vegetable or olive oil.

In Creole cooking, the proportions tend to be a matter of personal preference. The basis is one-to-one but slightly more flour may be added if the Roux seems too thin.

Roux not only thickens sauces, gravies and stocks but also adds an unmistakable undertone of taste.

Based upon the color of Roux the cook is producing, the tastes will vary. The three most common colors are blond, caramel (or peanut butter) and medium dark, or chocolate in color. All of the shades in between are common and simply occur by chance or by choice due to the length of cooking time and temperature.

A white Roux, which is the beginning of a Béchamel sauce, is not the same. It is cooked only a minute or two simply to cook out the flour taste before proceeding with the remaining steps of the sauce.

The most difficult Roux to produce is the darkest. Since it must be constantly stirred over a low flame for a long period of time, easily thirty minutes, there is a temptation to speed up the process by increasing the heat. That path will lead to certain failure. Once a Roux is scorched, it must be tossed and the cook must begin again.

A blond Roux should take five to 10 minutes, a medium Roux 15 to 20 minutes and the dark Roux as much as an hour, at a very low flame.

Plan the time carefully. Once a Roux has been started it must be constantly attended. The results are well worth the effort.

Creole cooks know that Roux will continue to cook in the pan once it is removed from the stove. The solution is to remove the pan from the flame shortly before the desired color is reached. Then proceed with the remainder of the recipe.

Basic Roux

YIELD: 3/4 TO 1 CUP OF ROUX

1/2 cup all-purpose flour
1/2 cup fat (depending on the recipe, the fat may be butter, clarified butter, bacon fat, vegetable or olive oil)

Use a heavy skillet, cast iron or other cast iron pot such as a Dutch oven based on the amount of Roux you are preparing. These pans will disperse the heat more slowly and evenly.

Place the chosen fat in skillet and heat over low flame. Begin adding the flour slowly, stirring continuously until all of the flour has been absorbed. As it is stirred, the texture will change, finally becoming a foamy mixture. Continue stirring until it has reached the desired color.

The Trinity

Chef's seasoning, Creole seasoning or chop-chop, as Arnaud's kitchen calls it, is nothing more than three simple vegetables in equal amounts.

This combination of onion, bell pepper and celery is cut into 1/2-inch dice.

Variations using colored bell peppers or red onions do not do much to affect taste levels but add color to the dish.

2 bell peppers, tops and membranes removed and seeded, cut into 1/2-inch dice
1 large onion, cut into 1/2-inch dice
4 stalks of celery cut into 1/2-inch dice

Combine, seal into a tub or zip lock bag and refrigerate until use. The Trinity can be added to a Roux and sauteed in it to stop it from becoming darker than desired. These seasonings add the kind of flavor and character that create the distinctive Creole taste.

Fresh Bouquet Garni

Bouquet garni is the French term for a bundle of fresh herbs tied together and tossed into the pot. It is then removed so the seasonings do not remain in the dish.

1/2 bunch parsley
3 bay leaves
1 sprig thyme
1 stalk celery, including tops, chopped

Enclose herbs or dry seasonings in a 7-inch square of cheesecloth; draw the four corners together at the top and tie into a little pouch. Or, use a tea ball if the quantity is small enough. Fish the pouch out with a slotted spoon and discard.

Dry Bouquet Garni

4 cloves
1 bay leaf
1 teaspoon black peppercorns
1 teaspoon dried thyme
1/2 teaspoon dried marjoram

Enclose herbs or dry seasonings in a 7-inch square of cheesecloth; draw the four corners together at the top and tie into a little pouch. Or, use a tea ball if the quantity is small enough. Fish the pouch out with a slotted spoon and discard.

Seasonings

Chefs started out to control recipe consistency by measuring and mixing their spices and herbs in advance and created a big business. Orleanians have always known about seasoning blends.

We take great delight in creating our personal batches of seasoned items including flour, oil, vinegar, butter and herb and spice mixtures. These are all easily purchased but it is much more satisfying to prepare your own.

It is best to prepare seasoning blends without salt, balancing sodium levels of the actual dish based on other ingredients (for the same reason that unsalted butter is generally preferred for cooking).

Work in small batches and store in tightly covered containers, since dried herbs lose their intensity over time. These colorful jars make excellent gifts.

Seafood Seasoning

YIELD: ABOUT 1/2 CUP OF DRY SEASONING MIXTURE PER RECIPE

2 tablespoons granulated garlic
2 tablespoons granulated onion
2 tablespoons freshly ground black pepper
1 teaspoon powdered oregano
1/2 teaspoon powdered thyme
1/2 teaspoon white pepper
1/4 teaspoon powdered basil
1/4 teaspoon Cayenne pepper

Mix dry ingredients together using a fork or place in a jar, cover and shake it thoroughly. Store in tightly covered container.

Poultry Seasoning

YIELD: ABOUT 1/2 CUP OF DRY SEASONING MIXTURE PER RECIPE

1 tablespoon Kosher or sea salt
1 teaspoon paprika
1/2 teaspoon onion powder
1/2 teaspoon garlic powder
1/2 teaspoon freshly ground black pepper
1/2 teaspoon freshly ground white pepper
1/2 teaspoon ground Cayenne pepper
1/2 teaspoon dried rosemary
1/2 teaspoon dried sage
1/2 teaspoon dried oregano
1/2 teaspoon dried thyme

Mix dry ingredients together using a fork or place in a jar, cover and shake thoroughly. Store in tightly covered container.

Creole Seasoning

YIELD: ABOUT 1/2 CUP OF DRY SEASONING MIXTURE PER RECIPE

3 tablespoons sweet paprika
2 tablespoons onion powder
2 tablespoons garlic powder
2 tablespoons dried oregano leaves
2 tablespoons dried sweet basil
1 tablespoon dried thyme leaves
1 tablespoon freshly ground black pepper
1 tablespoon freshly ground white pepper
1 tablespoon Cayenne pepper
1 tablespoon Kosher or sea salt
Dash of chili powder
Dash of cumin powder

Mix dry ingredients together using a fork or place in a jar, cover and shake thoroughly. Store in tightly covered container.

For Blackened Seasoning add an additional tablespoon each of paprika and Cayenne pepper for color and heat.

Creole Seasoned Flour

YIELD: 2-1/4 CUPS

2 cups all purpose flour
4 tablespoons paprika
1 tablespoon Kosher or sea salt
1 tablespoon garlic powder
1/2 tablespoons black pepper, ground
1/4 cup Cayenne pepper

Mix dry ingredients together using a fork or place in a jar, cover and shake thoroughly. Store in tightly covered container.

Seafood Fry

YIELD: 2-1/4 CUPS

1 cup masa (corn) flour
1 cup all-purpose flour
3 tablespoons Creole seasoning
1 tablespoon Kosher or sea salt

Mix dry ingredients together using a fork or place in a jar, cover and shake thoroughly. Store in tightly covered container.

The addition of 1/2 cup of corn starch to a flour mixture will make the fry extra crispy.

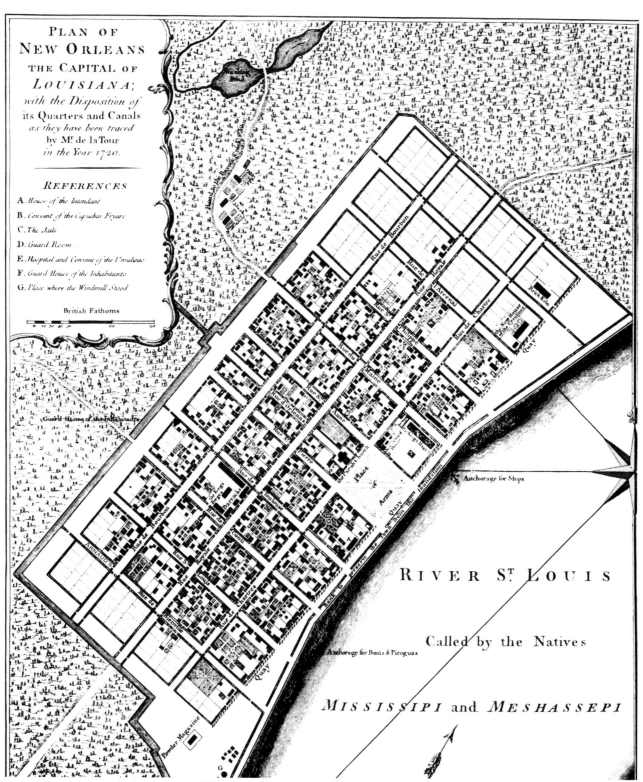

PLAN OF
NEW ORLEANS
THE CAPITAL OF
LOUISIANA;
with the Disposition of
its Quarters and Canals
as they have been traced
by Mr de la Tour
in the Year 1720.

REFERENCES

A. *House of the Intendant*
B. *Convent of the Capuchin Fryars*
C. *The Jails*
D. *Guard Room*
E. *Hospital and Convent of the Ursulines*
F. *Guard House of the Inhabitants*
G. *Place where the Windmill Stood*

British Fathoms

RIVER St LOUIS

Called by the Natives

MISSISSIPI and *MESHASSEPI*

The 1720 De la Tour map is the first survey that divides the blocks into numbered lots. The Mississippi River is titled St. Louis. Some of Arnaud's and Remoulade buildings are indicated. The map also shows the location of the powder magazine storage, which is now Magazine Street.

Index

Arnaud's Restaurant
813 Bienville Street
New Orleans, LA 70112
(504) 523-5433

http://www.arnauds.com

As Arnaud's grew each building was incorporated by simply removing walls between them. The original mosaic floors in different patterns identify the various structures.

Acknowledgements

Restaurants are fueled by people, staff and guests. The constant interplay creates the dynamic excitement of daily performances. There is a lot more than cooking going on behind the scenes.

Arnaud's staff had a major role in this production. Each is a first-rate professional, especially executive chef Tommy DiGiovanni, who answered countless questions with good humor and patience, along with sous chef José Manguia, pastry chef Cathy Pollard, Chico Plets, Joyce Barnes, Karen Terry, Lisa Sins, Debbie Ryall, Danny Robichaux, Charles Abbyad, Bobby Oakes and Bill Gillespie.

I also appreciate the support of Gene Bourg, retired *Times Picayune* restaurant critic, who can describe gumbo in more ways than anyone else in the world, and Tom Fitzmorris (aka Mr. Food), whose wit and words on his radio show, and in print, have sustained my appetite for the absurd through the years.

A special thanks to others who worked together so long, the late Edwin Williams, Jedd Haas, Ginny Warren, Susan Hennessey, Christine Mason, Hans Haveman, Michele Barker, Patty Fox, Robin Blut, Mickey Caplinger, Brigit Binns, David Spielman, Paul Rico and Lloyd Dobyns. The most important ingredient in any project is encouragement and for that, my great thanks go to Jane and Archie Casbarian, Linda Dennery, Julie Smith, Linda Ellerbee and Billy Wohl, my husband.